CULTURES IN CONVERSATION

LEA's COMMUNICATION SERIES
Jennings Bryant/Dolf Zillmann, General Editors

For a complete list of titles in LEA's Communication Series, please contact Lawrence Erlbaum Associates, Publishers at www. erlbaum.com

CULTURES IN CONVERSATION

Donal Carbaugh
University of Massachusetts

LAWRENCE ERLBAUM ASSOCIATES, PUBLISHERS
2005   Mahwah, New Jersey   London

Lawrence Erlbaum Associates, Inc., Publishers
10 Industrial Avenue
Mahwah, New Jersey 07430
www.erlbaum.com

Cover design by Sean Trane Sciarrone

Library of Congress Cataloging-in-Publication Data

Carbaugh, Donal A.
    Cultures in conversation / Donal Carbaugh.
    p. cm.
Includes bibliographical references and index.
ISBN 0-8058-5233-6 (cloth : alk. paper)
ISBN 0-8058-5234-4 (pbk. : alk. paper)
    1. Intercultural communication. 2. Conversation analysis. I. Title.

P94.6.C37 2005
302.2—dc22
                                        2004061424
    CIP

Books published by Lawrence Erlbaum Associates are printed on acid-free paper, and their bindings are chosen for strength and durability.

Printed in the United States of America
10 9 8 7 6 5 4 3 2

There are no worlds but other worlds...
Known or unknown, every world exists because others do.

—Wendell Berry

Contents

Table of Transcripts

Preface

Over the past few years, perhaps like you, I have found myself in various social scenes that were being creatively cast through conversations, as well as uniquely exhibiting cultures. Let me mention a few of the more memorable of these. In one, I was standing in, what seemed to me, a very public Finnish hospital space with my pants down around my knees while two female nurses administered a shot to my buttocks; similarly, after a wonderfully searing hot time in a Finnish sauna, I found myself walking across the early April snow, bare naked, in full view of anyone who wished to take notice. In Moscow, Russia, at Lenin's mausoleum in Red Square, I was castigated by Russian officers for walking into the shrine with my hands in my suit pockets and for talking to my Russian accomplice; or also in Russia, at Moscow State University, I ate breakfast with college athletes, enjoying hot dogs, mashed potatoes, a pickle, two slices of bologna and tea, while Gloria Estefan sang Salsa music over the speakers. On the northern plains of the U.S., in Blackfeet country, I found myself the only "whiteman" among Native people under a steamy dark dome of willow, while a Blackfeet participant prayed for "whitemen" who intrude where they don't belong; or I was walking with a Blackfeet colleague who informed me that a crow had just said something worthy of our attention. In Shanghai, China, on the steps of the National Museum, I quite unexpectedly met a female Finnish colleague who took me by the hands and began dancing the Tango with me, which delighted me to no end!

Moments as these provide memorable experiences, as social interactions cast us into scenes that are rich for thought, deep in their design, and stand at the juncture of multiple traditions. Scenes as these also invoke cultural worlds and customs for conduct, as conversations within them creatively shape the forms and meanings of those worlds and that conduct.

While these few introductory examples may seem overly exotic or unusual, the general process of conversing through cultures is not. At least this is what I seek to demonstrate: Cultures and conversations come together in our contemporary worlds, each woven into patterns of social practice, each intricately intertwined with the other in complex and sometimes vexing ways.

What do we say while we are involved in moments like these? What, then, can we say about them?

In this book, I build accounts of conversational interactions that seek to preserve their cultural shapes and meanings. In so doing, I have tried sedulously to render conversations through codes, that is, through the terms, sequences, and premises that are familiar to those who have created them. The idea is that people, to some degree and in some particular ways, make conversation what it is. They have some idea about what it is they are doing as they converse, and they do so in the particular ways they find effective and pleasing—or may critique as ineffective or displeasing. Can we come to understand conversation in this way, by keeping in view what people, on the ground, so to speak, have made of it? I think we can, even must, build such accounts, with participants' views of it in mind, with the studies assembled here demonstrating my efforts to do so.

A starting point in building such accounts is that conversation, and communication generally, is a kind of practical art, infused with people's tastes and habits. In analyzing and understanding it, we can work with those creations. As a result, we can turn our attention to the interactional practices of people in places, trying to grasp their sense of its significance and importance, their grounds for understanding its shapes and meanings. The objective is not simply to report what people say about conversations, although we should do some of that. The objective is further to formulate the meaningfulness of conversational interaction to participants in terms they find resonant, important to them, thereby opening portals into their communal standards for such action. Building accounts of conversation in this way—with serious attention to participants' accounts—we can re-enter conversational scenes, interpret the richness of its multiple contours, deepen our senses of how conversation is not only practiced by people, but moreover interpreting how it invokes larger worlds of meaning. If we are somehow successful in our efforts, participants can hear the account as somehow familiar to them, as resonant with their sense of the practice, yet moreover as informative, as saying something about the practice that had not been thought about quite that way before. In the process, we seek to honor participant's worlds of meaning, creating our accounts with them, thereby constructing through reflection, as through all practical art, a sense of the practice as motivated social interaction. With our fingers on peoples' pulses, ears tuned to their cultural chords, hearing an ethos for an ethnos, we seek to understand cultures in conversation.

Acknowledgments

I am indebted to many people who have helped in making the following studies not only possible, but pleasurable. I must mention the following: The studies in England were made possible by the kind invitation and support of Professor Rom Harré at Linacre College of the University of Oxford, England; the Finnish studies have been supported and funded variously by several members of the Fulbright Foundation, the American Center in Helsinki, the Universities of Helsinki, Jyvaskyla and Tampere, and the School of Business Administration and Economics at Turku, some of whom I will mention below; the Russian studies were aided by Anna Pavlovskaya and the Center for Cross-Cultural Studies at Moscow State University, and by Mikhail Makorov of Tver State University; the Blackfeet studies were advanced immeasurably with the help of a Jacob Research Grant from the Whatcomb Museum, Bellingham, Washington, and by crucial support from the Office of Research Affairs, the University of Massachusetts at Amherst. In addition to these people and institutions, many others have offered rich opportunities for discussion and direction and I must mention among these Nancy Aalto and Liisa Kurki-Suonio of the Language Centre at the University of Tampere, Finland; Michael Berry of the Turku School of Business Administration and Economics, Finland; Jaakko Lehtonen, Aino Sallinen, and Liisa Salo-Lee of the Department of Communication, University of Jyvaskyla, Finland; Marjatta Nurmikari-Berry of Turku Polytechnic, Finland; Jens Brockmeier of the Free University in Berlin and the University of Innsbruck, Austria; Elena Khatskevich of Buryatia, Russia, and the University of Massachusetts; Jack Gladstone, Hawkstone Productions, Kalispell, Montana; Darrel Norman (aka Buffalo Body) of the Lodge Pole Gallery and Tipi Village, Browning, Montana; Darrell Robes Kipp, Executive Director of the Piegan Institute, Browning, Montana; and Curly Bear Wagner of Heart Butte, Montana.

At the University of Massachusetts, I am fortunate to be part of an intellectual community in which conversation, cultures, and social interaction are being variously explored and studied. I am particularly grateful for the discussions being sustained in our graduate programs by many colleagues and students. My hope is that the following writings in some way contribute to these and related discussions.

Several others have provided insight, encouragement, and friendship during the rather long process of researching and writing this book. Among these, Gerry Philipsen stands out as a long-standing source of insight, inspiration, friendship, and support. Each of the following also has helped with their continuing interest and conversations: Pua Aiu, Betsy Bach, Benjamin Bailey, Charles Braithwaite, Connie Bullis, Mary Jane Collier, Leda Cooks, Lisa Coutu, Patricia Covarrubias, Vernon Cronen, Natalie Dollar, Donald Ellis, Kristine Fitch, Xinmei Ge, Tim Gibson, Phil Glenn, Daena Goldsmith, Brad Hall, Mitch Hammer, Sally Hastings, Michael Hecht, Tamar Katriel, Young Y. Kim, Judith Martin, Trudy Milburn, Eric Morgan, Stephen Olbrys, Lisa Rudnick, Max Saito, Robert Sanders, Michelle Scollo Sawyer, Robin Shoaps, Rebecca Townsend, Richard Wilkins, Karen Wolf Wilkins, and Michaela Winchatz.

About the Author

Donal Carbaugh is Professor of Communication at the University of Massachusetts, Amherst. His general interests focus on cultural philosophies of communication, and more specifically, the ways culturally distinctive practices get woven into international and intercultural interactions, with special attention to the relationship between language use, culture, spirit, and nature. His published research includes the book *Talking American: Cultural Discourses on DONAHUE* (1988), the edited volume *Cultural Communication and Intercultural Contact* (1990), and *Situating Selves: The Communication of Social Identities in American Scenes* (1996), *Narrative and Identity* (2001, edited with Jens Brockmeier). Recipient of a Hewlett Fellowship, a Fulbright Fellowship, an Advanced Institute of the Humanities Fellowship, and several grants, he has enjoyed lecturing across the United States, Europe, and Asia.

Introduction

Cultures in Conversation is written to introduce readers to the ethnographic study of intercultural and social interactions. This is done by analyzing several specific conversations in which different cultural orientations are operating, seeking to hear in them, cultures at work. The particular cases analyzed and commented on involve conversations that bring together practices from Britain, Finland, Russia, Blackfeet Country, and the United States, with each being in some sense distinctive in its communication codes, that is, in its use of symbolic meanings, forms, norms, and motivational themes. Treating conversation in this way, focusing on intercultural interactions, is an effort to demonstrate how cultural lives are active in conversation, in different ways, and to show how conversation is a principal medium for the coding of selves, social relationships, and societies. Eventually, the following inquiries will bring into view features of intercultural and social interaction, through microdetails of talk, which are variously mediated, while invoking macronotions of culture as well. As a result, cultures are being understood as active in conversations, just as conversations are understood to activate cultures. My hope is the integrative spirit of such inquiry may invite others to further examine ethnographic inquiry as a way of studying intercultural conversations in particular, and communication practices in general.

Many readers are undoubtedly aware of "conversation analysis" (or CA) as a widely adopted approach to the study of conversation. The works of CA have assumed a prominent and particular view of "conversation" (from the view of the CA tribe) and "talk-in-interaction." As recent discussions by Emmanuel Schegloff and Michael Billig in *Discourse and Society* (1999) show, however, there are different approaches possible in the study of conversation. My aim is to use and demonstrate a cultural view, to show how social interaction involves cultural features including its sequential shapes, meanings, and motivations. From my standpoint, an ethnographic approach adds a distinctive and complementary view to these matters, unveiling conversation as something deeply cultural, and demonstrating this point with intercultural encounters (see e.g., Carbaugh, 1990a, 1990c, 1993c; Philipsen 1987, 1997, 2002). I work, then, to bring into view an order of organization that is different from that featured in "conversation analysis." Where CA focuses on sequential organization that is identified by analysts and intersubjectively meaningful to participants, I seek to highlight a cultural organization that is identifiable by participants as part of the intersubjective meaningfulness of their interactions. Both are important orders of organization. If CA provides a kind of engineering, in parts and parcels, then the cultural view adopted here is a kind of biology, in ethos systems and fields. Both are undoubtedly active in conversations. Neither can be reduced to the other without transforming the claims being made. I see these views, then, as distinctive, and at times overlapping, while offering complementary approaches to the study of conversations, including intercultural encounters.

*****

In a recent survey of intercultural communication, Jan Blommaert (1998) observed that studies of "intercultural communication" were not offering what he expected. He reported:

> The study of empirical cases is not at the core of what many people understand by studies of intercultural communication. Quite a few well-known and widely read books on intercultural communication do not provide a single real case analysis, not even a single example of real-life data of people talking to one another. (p. 1)

Being asked to speak to audiences interested in the subject, Blommaert noted how "very few ... were actually concerned with the study of communication, very few with the study of culture" (p. 1). Blommaert's expressed frustration was a result, he claimed, of the paucity of research focused on actual communication practices in which cultural differences are apparent, and active. Blommaert is in company with others who have made a similar observation (Gudykunst & Ting-Toomey, 1988; Leeds-Hurwitz, 1990). By focusing on actual intercultural interactions, and doing so through culturally informed analyses of conversation, this book seeks to begin filling that gap.

*****

In the early spring of 1993, during an extended period of study in Finland, my family and I were invited to visit our friends, Liisa and

Allu, for "coffee." Late in the afternoon, our young children were gathered together upstairs playing rather quietly, as we sat together downstairs, looking out a picture window at a beautiful tranquil scene of snow-covered lake, blue sky, and pine trees. After several minutes of sitting in silence together, our friend, Liisa, turned to my wife and me and asked:

"When you are with your friends in the United States, do you talk most all of the time?" My wife and I looked at each other, nodded, and smiled, while I responded: "Well, uhm, yes, pretty much." Liisa said: "How do you do that? That must be exhausting!" We all laughed as my wife and I admitted, "Yeah, at times, it can be."

This conversation is a very brief example of the kind of moment being explored in this book. In it, people are interacting together, and as part of that process, they produce a conversation. In this case, the topic of the conversation is a possible cultural difference in the uses of conversation and silence. Liisa is wondering aloud if conversation in the United States occurs "most all of the time, when you are with your friends." She is asking, rather implicitly, if there is, among friends in the United States, little time given to being silent together—as we were, prior to her question, being. If little time is given to this kind of "quietude" and one were expected to talk "most all of the time," she imagines this to be "exhausting."

Liisa's comment and query directly implies, by contrast, something about Finnish conversation: That, at times, it might not involve so much talk, in the same way; that it might involve extended periods of quiet or silence, unlike what she has heard about American conversation. Her comment thus invites reflection on the silent form of sociable interaction we had been enjoying together prior to her question (in Finland), and its possible absence (in the United States).

Our brief moment of conversation had thus drawn into it—through the topic discussed and its enactment—cultural features of social interaction. These were not only being discussed, but also performed, here, in a uniquely Finnish way. In other words, sitting in silence together on this occasion was not just a social practice we were doing, but also, in this case, a cultural exigence for Liisa's asking about USAmerican "talk with your friends." Together in silence, we had created a social scene in which conversation and silence itself became relevant as topics for discussion, a Finnish period of quietude being a cause for reflecting on its cultural and conversational absence (in the United States). In the process, we brought to the fore, in response to Liisa's question, some sense of a difference. Liisa, Allu, and others in Finland of course enjoy conversing with others, yet also enjoy being silent with friends, as we were doing. They have been told, or have seen on television, or have realized firsthand while visiting in the United

States that this activity may be done differently there, where people apparently "talk all the time."

In conversations like these, then, what is the source of this expressed, and performed difference in speaking and silence? What cultural life does each have? How can acts of conversation and silences within it, as well as participants' beliefs about them, help us understand cultures in conversation? These are the kinds of questions being asked in this book.

In so inquiring, we seek to demonstrate both how culture is active in conversation, and, the dynamics that transpire when different cultural practices are active in the same occasion. By exploring this way, we move from a view of conversation as "talk-in-interaction," to a consideration of the role of culture in interactional sequences, to "moves" within interaction that create culturally distinct scenes, including acts other than "talk," such as nonlinguistic moves in communication, sometimes from nonhuman agents. The Finnish and Blackfeet materials among others warrant this treatment of the subject. In the end, these writings seek to demonstrate what an ethnographic approach to communication can contribute to studies of culture and interaction generally, and to Wendell Berry's observation in the opening quotation, that "every world exists because others do."

(IN)VISIBLE MISUNDERSTANDINGS

As people from different communities come together, they seek to coordinate their actions, and render meaningful those interactions. Typically, participants assume they understand what they are doing and what this means. However, there are times when the understandings of each, while presumably shared, in fact, are not being shared. For example, in Finnish scenes like the one just mentioned, a Finnish practice may involve a "harmonious quietude," and presume others are so acting, yet an other may deem that very action to be an "uncomfortable silence." As each presumes the other shares a frame of reference, together they may misunderstand each other. This kind of dynamic—assuming a shared meaning for interaction while acting into different, unshared events—can easily go unnoticed. I call this process, the movement from unknown and unshared, to known and potentially shareable frames of reference, *(in)visible (mis)understandings*. The phrase is a way of capturing movement in conversations from actual invisible misunderstandings to potentially visible understandings.

John Gumperz (1982) wrote classic studies that draw attention to such moments. As East Asian workers in a cafeteria in London served English customers, they would ask the customers if they wanted "gravy," but ask with falling rather than rising intonation. While this falling contour of sound signaled a question in Hindi, to English ears it sounded like a command. The servers thus were heard by British listeners to be rude and inappropriately bossy, when the server was simply trying to ask, albeit in a Hindi way, a question. In situations like these, one's habitual conversational practices can cue unwitting misunderstandings, yet those cues are typically beyond the scope of one's reflection. As a result, miscommunication is created, but in a way that is largely invisible to participants. Once known to them, communication can take a different form.

Benjamin Bailey (2000) studied social interactions similarly, in convenience stores in Los Angeles. He found that Korean storekeepers served clients through a particular sequence of a brief greeting, transacting the business at hand, then closing the transaction. This sequence works smoothly, especially with Korean-American customers. However, when African-American clients entered the scene, another sequence was noticed involving more verbal engagement, sometimes telling jokes, talking about the weather, asking about arrangements of goods in the store, as well as discussing one's activities generally. Through this sequential order, African-American customers sought more verbal engagement from Korean-American storekeepers. In reaction, the Korean-American storekeepers attempted to employ their preferred sequence, a three-part sequence of "restraint." Each act sequence, the Korean and African-American, is differently and unknowingly linked to deeply different norms of respectful communication, and thus each, largely unknowingly, exhibits disrespect for the other, all the while conducting their transactions as they think they should. As the other participant's preferences go unmet, so do misunderstandings arise. Through this process of what might be called "parallel sequential tracking" of cultural actions, confusions of symbolic meanings arise, forms of alignment are crossed, and expressed motivations get misread from one about the other.

The following studies, among other things, explore the kind of dynamics John Gumperz (1982) and Benjamin Bailey (2000) draw to our attention. In so doing, they apply and develop a cultural approach to conversation and social interaction. While invisible sources of miscommunication become noticed and highlighted, so to are explicit demonstrations of miscommunication explored.

PLAN OF THE BOOK

The following two chapters explore and demonstrate the idea that culture can be understood as part and parcel of conversation. The first chapter introduces the general approach and procedures followed in the studies. The second introduces various materials including an intercultural conversation in an English pub, and within it, conversational moves being made that exhibit different cultural premises about class, social hierarchy, equality, and personality. Similarly, an exchange between Russian and USAmerican business professors demonstrates the links between conversational acts and cultural premises with special attention to goals, motivations, and means of expression. Finally a Finnish story is discussed, which shows how conversational uses of narratives can construct and play with culturally distinctive styles of communicating. The chapter thus discusses how conversation both presumes and activates cultural premises of identity, action, sequences, affect, and rules.

Chapters 3 and 4 focus on Finnish and USAmerican (i.e., practices prominent and potent in some scenes of the United States) interactions through a third-party introduction, interactional sources of cultural stereotypes, and ways speakers present cultural typifications of others during a televised event. The third-party introduction involves Finnish and American practices, demonstrating how conversation is a cultural event punctuated by speaking and silence, including various cultural uses and meanings of the silences. Explored further are Finnish cultural premises that are active when identifying "Americans" as "superficial," a common attribution in Finland and northern Europe generally. Such assessments involve presumed links between interactional events, uses of superlatives, and rules for proper conversational conduct. Finnish and USAmerican premises as these are shown to be active in a prominent televised text, which presumes, plays with, and reproduces some of the interactional sources of these specific cultural typifications, of Finns and people from the United States.

Chapter 5 explores how Russian and USAmerican conversation involves ritual forms and sequences concerning "sex talk." When active simultaneously, these can create face threats as well as subsequent acts that seek, in their own ways, to restore a proper "expressive order," to use Goffman's (1967, p. 9) phrase. Hearing conversation as ritualized draws to our attention several features: (a) the cultural sequencing of acts, (b) specific cultural terms being used, (c) the lexical structuring of the topic, (d) the tone of the discussion, and (e) folk genres of talk that these at once presume, create, and resist. Cultural variation in these shows deeper meanings about proper conversation itself and what it means to be a person.

Chapter 6 and chapter 7 introduce a Blackfeet way of "listening" as an indigenous form of communication. Some features of this form are shown to be active in a classroom where public speaking is being taught. The form is complex, for it activates a range of cultural agents as possible participants in conversational activities, presumes a special link to physical places, and ignites nonlinguistic channels of conversational practice, albeit in culturally distinctive ways. While "listening" can involve spiritual meanings, it can also be understood as a way of giving proper time to what is presumably already present in social and physical space, to proper ways of understanding that space itself, including the various relations which the "listening" act and sequence presumes while there.

The final chapter of the book again brings to the fore the basic framework at work in it, focusing on the way cultural conversations provide interactional resources for expressing communal identity through specific communication practices, with these including cultural premises for social action and being a person. Communication, as such, is being discussed and interpreted as a metasocial commentary about action, the person, social relations, feeling, and dwelling in place. Interpreting conversation in this way provides a deeper way of understanding its sequential and symbolic qualities, generally. More specifically, the chapter summarizes the four cultural conversations at play in the book, the U.S. "self," the Russian "soul," the Finnish "silence," and the Blackfeet "spirit." Discussion centers on these rich symbols, the forms of practice each makes particularly relevant, the motivational themes presumed for each, and premises for personhood that are activated through each. And thus, culture and conversation are brought together, as are people's practices, each capable of informing the other.

COMPOSITION AND COOPERATION

Writing this book has been a long, collaborative process, which has followed many years of fieldwork. In putting these words on paper, I have been ever mindful of highly particular people and practices. In other words, as I sit to write, I constantly hear particular social occasions, deeply cultural scenes, in which people are conducting their lives together. In so doing, these scenes bring into view what people consider significant and important to them, doing what they do in ways they recognize as their own. So, as I struggled to understand their (and my) design for our conversations, I shared my thoughts in these scenes with them. Reactions were always instructive, for they led me deeper into the collective premises for what was going on, these being at times quite far from what I could have understood, initially, without their input.

Yet as I listen and consider the social interactional concerns in this book, and take seriously the comments made about them by those familiar with them, I am deeply engaged in a cooperative and collaborative activity of composition. And while lay folk are not always the best judges of their social interactional conduct, they are not to blame for any inadequacies in what follows, for their input has always been helpful in developing my understandings of the cultural bases of these practices, including the range of meanings and significance at play.

So, as I listened and wrote, I constantly sought the input of those whose practices I was trying to understand. In the end, after putting my thoughts on paper, I have always shared what I have come to understand with others, many of whom are now long-standing acquaintances and friends. I have been delighted when others have seen some value in these written thoughts, and have only published them after they passed this kind of test. And of course, along the way I have occasionally missed the mark, and with help have found a better way. Each chapter composition that follows has thus been co-produced with, read by, and presented in public (and private) to those who participate in such practices. Each principal part has also been published in outlets readily available to those cooperative others. Let me fill in some specifics to illustrate this process.

An earlier version of chapter 2 was presented as a keynote address at a large international conference with people from about 25 nations. Prominent in the audience were British, Russian, and Finnish participants, and thus my focus on those practices in that chapter. Reactions to my remarks, there, were instructive to me, and served to deepen my analyses of the interactional practices discussed in chapter 2. For example, after my address, a Russian scholar was speaking about bases of kinship and stressing the role of "blood" in conceptions of kinship relations. As he spoke, he assumed the stance and manner I had discussed in my address. Several audience members, especially Russian audience members, sought me out to say how my address helped bring this expressive style to their attention, involving its critical reflection. Similarly, the Finnish story about the American professor was repeatedly mentioned as an expression of differences in cultural styles of teaching. The chapter thus has been co-produced with others, with its parts being a source of discussion by those invested in those parts, all serving as aids in my comprehension and composition.

Chapter 3 has been co-authored with a Finnish student and colleague of mine, Saila Poutiainen. Her words in the composition help capture a Finnish sense of the conversational dynamics at play in it. Also, the segment of conversation displayed there has been shown and analyzed by me dozens of times over a decade in Finland to Finnish audiences (and in the United States to U.S. audiences). Reactions to these presentations have served to clarify and confirm what I present there. Similarly, chapter 4 is a version of an essay published in Finland for a Finnish audience, and was immediately reprinted in a popular outlet there. As a result, these studies are results of cooperative and collaborative, and sometimes contentious efforts, a process of researching various cultural insights, over the years.

Chapter 5 has been reprinted and translated into Russian, in a journal published by the Russian Academy of Sciences. In fact, discussing this work in Russia, in former Soviet Republics, and with Russian immigrants in the United States and Israel, has served to deepen my appreciation of the practices discussed there. Subsequent and related work has also been published by colleagues in outlets including the *Moscow Times*. Each publication, presentation, and performance of the work has thus seriously considered and treated themes important to, and resonant with, those whose practices are being recounted here.

Chapters 7 and 8 are more long-term in their development, considering as they do Native American, Blackfeet practices that have been difficult, initially, for me to grasp. This process has involved many discussions and presentations to nonnative and native friends and audiences, seeking to understand the motives and premises at play in them. I will never forget an encounter at our national convention when a teacher at a college asked if I had a few moments for a Native American student of hers. Of course I did. The student explained how she had read chapter 6, how it had for the first time made sense of her dual cultural household, and as a result, the chapter had "changed her life." She thanked me for writing it, but the thanks, from my view, was due to her. Although unanticipated, her remark among others has deeply touched and motivated me to further explorations that are ongoing.

This process of practicing ethnography in the field, living with people and trying to understand their practices—from their view—that we weave together, hearing what is made of my early and later accounts, and using all such input in the cooperative process of writing, lies at the heart of this book. As a result, it seeks an allegiance not just to a scholarly audience, although it does that, but also to cultural communities whose practices it seeks to understand. So, it is not just conversation and interaction of concern to us here, but cultures as well, as they structure, animate, struggle with, and thus give deeper shapes and shades to conversation itself, and the worlds it makes possible.

A NOTE ON IDENTIFYING TERMS

Throughout this volume, I identify practices by terms such as a Russian practice, a Finnish phrase, a Blackfeet mode, a USAmerican style. In each case, my objective is to identify a practice or feature of a practice that is prominent within, and distinctive of, some scenes of each society. Each of the identifying terms, then, draws attention to qualities of some interactive practices in a society; the claim thus applies to a class of practice, not to a population of people.

⋙ 1 ⋘

Cultures in Conversation: Ethnographic
Explorations of Intercultural Communication

What can the study of conversation tell us about the shapes and meanings of cultural worlds? In turn, what can the study of cultural worlds tell us about the shapes and meanings of conversation? As Michael Moerman (1988) wrote, "In every moment of talk, people are experiencing and producing their cultures, their roles, their personalities" (p. xi). How can we understand these moments of talk, as means of producing roles, personalities, and cultures, that is, as ways of crafting ourselves and ways of living together?

This book responds to these questions by exploring moments of talk, and hearing in them participants' ways of being and living together. Based on various studies of these moments, along with others, I have been developing a position through which such a study can be productively done. To begin, I provide a brief formulation of that stance, which is introduced here: Conversation is indeed, typically, about topics, and occurs between people as a more or less improvisational yet structured activity. Conversation can be understood also as a symbolic phenomenon, as a kind of metasocial commentary—whether intended or not—about the activities we are doing, about who we are, how we are related to each other, how we feel about what is going on, and the nature of the situation. In some sense, then, in every conversation, one or more cultures is at work, if by culture we are drawing attention to symbolic phenomena that say something about our common senses of acting (what we are doing together and how we do it), of being (who we are), of relating (how we are linked to each other), of feeling (about people, actions, and things), and of dwelling together (how we relate to the world around us). Conversation is worthwhile, then, indeed even significant and important, at least partly because in it are deep sensibilities about acting, being, relating, feeling, and dwelling, respectively; that is, what is meaningful in our lives together. This book demonstrates this complex thesis through a series of studies about moments of talk and interaction.

A BASIC UNIT: CULTURE IN CONVERSATION

Analyzing cultural features as inherent in conversation is no easy task, for analyses as these demand traveling a two-way street. Just as culture inhabits conversations, so too does conversation inhabit cultures. There is a part–whole relation active in studying this interactive terrain, with every conversational part being part and parcel of a larger system of cultural meaning, just as the larger system of meaning can bring into view particular features of the conversational parts. As a result, attention is sustained on "talk-in-interaction-in-culture," or "culture-in-interaction-in-talk," the basic unit being at once a conversational part as part and parcel of a cultural system of expression, each serving as a resource for understanding the other. Thus, in conversation, we find particular expressions of symbolic meanings (i.e., culture-in-conversation), just as in culture, we find symbolic interaction through its conversational parts (i.e., conversation-in-culture).

This two-way street can become quite busy, for as we travel it, we can hear the sounds of conversation and culture, we can notice different vehicles, or different parts on the same vehicle. Now and then, we might see a car with two different fenders, one from a Ford, the other from a Toyota. In other words, a conversational vehicle can be designed with different cultural parts. A vehicle of expression can be understood with its multifaceted features, bringing different shapes, and/or meanings into the symbolic street. This occurs as conversation is being crafted with different cultural tools—a Geertzian (or Rylesian) blink is taken by another as a wink—with both remaining active in the subsequent exchange. In the process, one conversational part may become interactionally divisible as a parcel of different actional and ideational sequences, that is, the symbolic play of intercultural conversations.

Something like this happens, for example, as a Chinese form of negotiation presumes a meaning of "support." Yet, when used with Dutch interlocutors, this Chinese action of "support" can escape their notice. The Chinese signaling of support is not typically visible (nor audible) from within the Dutch "car" of negotiation. As a result, Dutch interlocutors can look to Chinese to be, unknowingly to them, not driving in a properly "supportive" way (Li & Koole, 1998). As Chinese continue to signal and turn onto the road of support, the Dutch move along, inattentive to this central feature in the Chinese landscape. Proper subsequent action, then, from the vantage of the Chinese expressive system, which should and presumably would play its role within a larger supportive sequence, goes unnoticed, unremarked, and undone by the Dutch! Chinese acts of support, and Chinese acts designed to elicit "support," thus play out in a particular Chinese way, but are beyond the notice of the Dutch discourse, which carries on beyond or over this act, through its own system of expression, sequence, and significance. One understands conversational parts as these, here and there, and the role they play, by their place in some larger whole(s). Envisioning conversational acts this way, one can eventually come to an understanding of how specific parts of conversational and cultural activity are geared to different sequences, and different symbolic messages, with different expressive systems being deemed central to the conduct of each part.[1]

At any one juncture between conversational systems, one act might seem nearly unrecognizable to others, being important to some but not all that central to what (other) participants orient to, as what-they-believe-for-the-moment is going on. In other words, at times, there are, at this juncture, conversational acts being introduced from different cultural discourses (from different configurations of an act–sequence system), this demonstrating how alternate ways of living are active (see Burke, 1965). Here, of course, our spatial analogy might break down a bit, because any one conversational part can play a role in two expressive systems at the same time, as when a greeting in silence may be more recognizable in one expressive system (e.g., a Finnish one) than in another (e.g., in some communities of the United States), making such an act possibly active—even in different ways—in both systems. Understanding interactional workings as these are the very objective of a comparative conversation analysis, as conversational parts simultaneously play into various sequences and expressive systems, deliberately bringing both the conversational parts and the cultural orientations of the participants into view.

CULTURES IN CONVERSATION: AN ETHNOGRAPHIC AND COMPARATIVE PERSPECTIVE

The following chapters feature prominent and popular cultural paths of conversations in several symbolic and geographic regions: the United States, Finland, Russia, England, and Blackfeet country (Montana, United States). Of particular concern are conversational moments in which one prominent and at times dominant U.S. expressive system contacts those of an other. I focus on these moments in order to achieve several aims: (a) an understanding of intercultural communication as an interactive practice; (b) an exploration of how some conversational practices, on these occasions, form parts of different expressive systems; (c) to present some of the cultural premises, or deeper meanings, which are active in those practices; (d) to contribute to our understanding of both interactional and communicational dynamics in such moments, (e) and to do so by careful attention to the details and cultural significance of those interactional sequences. My objectives are both highly specific, in bringing conversation into view as a particular system of cultural expression, and general, to help construct a view of conversation that is sensitive to cultural variability.[2]

The range of conversational phenomena explored in the following essays is quite broad. It includes, as examples, structuring norms for conversation in an English pub, various cultural goals from speaking the truth to espousing virtues in public settings, social uses of narratives that contrast cultural styles of speaking, the role of silence in third-party introductions and in other communication events, cultural rules for conducting oneself in communication events generally, ritualized forms and norms for interactional sequencing, as well as various cultural means of identifying and structuring talk itself. The latter draw to our attention indigenous terms for communicative actions, for example Finnish "tutustua taloon" (i.e., getting acquainted with an academic department or literally, "the house"), Russian "poshum dusa" ("soul talk"), a Blackfeet form of "listening," and popular U.S. forms of "being honest" and "sharing one's feelings." Each exploration seeks to interpret these phenomena as conversational and cultural phenomena, as sequential and symbolic phenomena. Further, each is systemic, with each part being a part in larger expressive systems.

Leaning on the idea that communicative activities like these are for the most part—but not always—meaningful activities to participants, following others, I formulate that meaningfulness with the concept of *cultural premise*. With it we ask: what are the basic beliefs that are being presumed for this action to be what it is, to be organized as it is? What is it that participants believe to be getting done? Given this, what is presumably valued as better or worse? Analyses as these draw attention to particular cultural features of, and in conversation, akin to what John Gumperz (1992) described as "conversational inference ... the situated or context-bound process of interpretation by which participants in an exchange retrieve relevant background knowledge and assess others' communicative intentions" (p. 306). Through this interpretive process, conversants identify and orient to the kinds of acts getting done, thereby putting their acts together in particular sequences. What gets accomplished is a kind of "contextualization," a linking of conversational parts to larger activities that are presumably, to participants, for now, relevant. Cultural premises, then, are formulations of particular beliefs (and values) that are in conversational activity, and about conversational activity; they are an analyst's rendering of what is presumably cultural in conversation. When formulated, cultural premises of belief and value—in and about conversation—provide a way of talking about the deeper, often taken-for-granted meaningfulness of expressive acts and sequences to participants, a typically unspoken yet expressively active resource for the practices to be indeed what they are. Cultural premises are, therefore, in sum, analysts' formulations of conversants' beliefs about the significance and importance of what is going on, both as a condition for that practice of conversation, and as expressed in that very practice (cf. Carbaugh, 1990a; Fitch, 1994, 1998; Geertz, 1973; Philipsen, 1997).

Formulating the premises in these expressive practices allows us in turn to address explicitly what is cultural in conversational acts and sequences. For example, in chapter 4, we explore how USAmerican questions of fact (e.g., "Are girls virgins when they marry?") are met with Russian replies about virtues (e.g., "Girls should be virgins when they marry"). Understanding the expressive system that each activates—of which each is a part—and premises for each, can help us understand the kind of cultural action getting done when questions of fact meet replies about virtues, as well as the significance of this interactional event within a USAmerican and Russian coding of conversation. Comparatively analyzing conversation in this way brings into view different premises for the enactment of conversational acts and sequences, and for the interpretation of its meanings to participants.

The explorations into these matters have been created over a number of years and are influenced by many people, places, and ways of thinking. My assumptions about communication, conversation, and speech are deeply influenced by the scholarly program initiated by John Gumperz and Dell Hymes (1962, 1972), and taken up, among many others by Benjamin Bailey (2000), Keith Basso (1996), Richard Bauman (1986), Patricia Covarrubias (2002), Kristine Fitch (1998), Dell Hymes (1996), Tamar Katriel (2004), Gerry Philipsen (1992), David Samuels (2001), Ron and Suzanne Scollon (1995), Joel Sherzer (1987), Deborah Tannen (1984, 1986) and Greg Urban (1991). Without denying the general status of certain conversational sequences and structures, these authors have helped make it abundantly clear that localized situations and communities have their own ways of conceiving, evaluating, and conducting communication.[3]

The following studies seek to demonstrate and make some small contribution to ethnographic explorations of conversation. More specifically, noting that the program Hymes envisioned was explicitly comparative, we might cast the following studies as exercises in a *comparative conversation analysis,* a kind of cross-cultural analysis of the means and meanings—as Hymes has put it—of conversation. In terms of the theory of cultural communication, the following studies place cultural conversations in comparative perspective, exploring how different codes for living are being realized in social interaction (Philipsen, 1987, 2002). Designed this way, we are exploring comparatively moments of conversation, acts of talk in sequence and in symbolic systems, by placing in cross-cultural perspective the cultural premises for the structuring of those very acts (Carbaugh, 1990a, 1990c).

The specific approach I assume stands at the juncture of communication codes theory (Philipsen, 1997) and cultural discourse theory (Carbaugh, Gibson, & Milburn, 1997). *Communication* is understood as a cultural practice, within processes of social interaction, with accounts of that practice being created by positing speech codes and cultural discourses, that is, the premises for conceiving and conducting conversation. The approach shares with practical theory a focus on metadiscourse as an everyday and theoretical concern (Carbaugh, 1989; Craig, 1999a&b; Taylor, 1997), and with *phronetic social science,* a focus on the particularities of value-rational action (Flyvbjerg, 2001).

INVESTIGATIVE MODES AND PROCEDURES: DISCOVERING, DESCRIBING, AND INTERPRETING

The following studies seek to capture something deemed important to participants in their intercultural, conversational conduct. Each has involved distinct investigative modes: discovering something about conversation, describing instances of this, and interpreting cultural premises, rules, and forms for these conversational practices.

What is **discovered** are specific conversational phenomena that are in some sense general, but are being used in particular and revealing ways, such as the composition and interpretation of superlatives, silence, introductory or interview sequences. Each conversational moment as this was **described** as it was created in some interactional context(s). Effort was given to recording such moments, making a record that could be examined in detail, and made public. The cultural workings of the conversation then were also **interpreted,** presenting some of the meaning and significance of these phenomena to participants as they are active in conversation. In this sense, the following comparative analyses of conversation follow moments of discovery and observation of conversational phenomena, with descriptive and interpretive analyses of their use and meanings.

The general procedure I followed when conducting these studies involved distinct phases of inquiry, which move, through comparative study, from descriptive to interpretive claims. First, I focused, within my general corpora of data, on a particular moment of social practice in which two cultural expressive systems were apparently active. Second, usually with the aid of collaborators, I created a careful record of that moment, and generated a collection of other like moments. Third, again with the help of consultants, I identified the conversational features of that moment, which yielded some understanding of that social interaction, from the point of view of the cultural actors. Finally, I interpreted the codes and discourses that explicated the cultural premises concerning the conception, enactment, and significance of those parts. The first step deserves some further comment.[4]

The first step involved creating a descriptive record of a kind of social interaction in which cultures were featured in conversation. For example, in the next chapter I analyze a particular kind of conversation I found myself co-producing while at Oxford, England. After puzzling over its fairly regular occurrence, I began recording further instances of this kind in my field journal. Presented in the text is one such transcription of this kind of recording. Similarly, while in Finland, I repeatedly found myself being introduced by a third party to others, eventually realizing that this event was being conducted in cultural ways and thus began recording those events. Chapter 3 includes a transcription and analyses of one of these events. Further, with Russian immigrants in the United States, I found similar forms and sequences of talk active and thus recorded these in various settings, leading to the selection of a televised demonstration of these dynamics for analysis. A transcription of this event appears in chapter 5. And so on. What I want to emphasize is this: Each transcription presented in what follows is a selection from a collection, or an instance from a corpus of data upon which the analyses rest. Although the prose in this volume is written around particular transcriptions of moments of talk, the analyses presented are based upon a larger corpus of data of similar instances that, in each case, were collected and analyzed during a lengthy fieldwork period, including extended discussions with my consultants in the field.

Part of the task of the following analyses is thus the recording for public display of something that indeed did happen. The transcriptions provide a kind of descriptive claim, then, of an actual moment of conversational practice that actually occurred among participants. What it was that happened, however, is partly a question for analysis, because answering the "what?" question, puts one—frequently but not always—in a domain of identifying something as an instance of a kind of action, and doing that assigns some significance and value to it. That process, of discovering, describing, and categorizing, as I present it, seeks to keep in view one "order of conversational organization," a cultural order, thereby interpreting acts, moves, sequences, rules, forms, and their meanings on the basis of a descriptive record, and with allegiance to the perspective of the participants in the talk itself. In that sense the interpretive claims I work toward, on the basis of the descriptive records, draw attention to the intersubjective meaningfulness of the conversational practice to participants, themselves, using whenever possible, their terms and meanings for those practices. Discovering, then, that the cawing of a crow or a lengthy silence were codable parts of a social interaction, and thus fodder for the transcriptional exercise, became part of the investigative process itself. It is not as if "the talk" itself is there for the inspection. What it is that is being fixed in transcriptive form is part of the findings, fixed in the terms of some community, whether academic and/or other. I think this is inevitable. Recognizing this provides a way of keeping the descriptive and interpretive accounts as close to the participants' meaningfulness of the "talk" as is possible.[5]

COMPARATIVELY ANALYZING CONVERSATIONAL RESOURCES: MOVES, CHANNELS, AND SEQUENCES

Each investigation that follows explores resources of conversation as parts of expressive systems. For example, one question I pose was suggested when, what I thought were compliments, were being heard by some Finns as rather "excessive praise" (cf. Pomerantz, 1978). When exploring what constituted a well-formed compliment and what action was being proposed as such, I found a superlative form being used by a USAmerican speaker in reference to freshly baked bread: "That's really wonderful!" At the time of its utterance I sensed something had been expressed to Finnish hearers beyond my own ability to understand. Eventually, with the help of my Finnish friends, I realized how this utterance was being experienced as two different cultural moves, and thus came to know how this utterance, its action and sequential use, was being cast quite differently in the two expressive systems: Within one USAmerican system, the presumed action was a fine compliment; within the Finnish system, the utterance was experienced as an overstatement. The same sequential use of one superlative expression was making reference to one state of affairs (i.e., the freshly cooked bread), yet the same referring form—"that's really wonderful"—created different actions regarding those affairs. The various actions (from sincere praise to overstatement), emotional affects (from fondness to skepticism), and the social relations being forged (from close to distant), were being presumed and expressed through this one superlative form, with this form (the act and its sequential structure) being understood differently, depending on the larger expressive system(s) of which it was deemed a part.

In a similar vein, silence will be explored as a communicative action, full of meaning, demonstrating how the "same" act of silence can vary, as when, on an occasion, it can signify for some, deep respect, whereas for others, defiance. Both examples, of superlatives and silence, suggest how conversational parts, in intercultural moments generally, are composed as interactional moves within different cultural sequences, with each expressive game differently positioning each part, even transforming earlier parts through the subsequent movement of the games. What sometimes results is a puzzling, even dazzling dynamic, as if a lob over the net is met with a slam dunk! In this sense, specific acts are typically composed as if they are parts of larger conversational sequences and systems, and when there is reverberation between systems, each with its own premises, what can result is a considerable discordant symphony between different cultural scores in a single improvised concert, as if Bach and Yanni are together playing bolero in the tempo of jazz.

How and when should one initiate a conversation? Should one get to know others before talking with them? And if one converses, what sequential structure holds integrity for participants? When conversing, what obligations does one incur given one's participation? For some, a conversation incurs an obligation to converse again, upon a subsequent meeting. For others, an initial conversation does not forge this obligation in the same way. What work is getting done in conversational parts and plays, and how do these relate to subsequent interactional sequences, use of various channels, and expressive moves?

If it is the case that conversation presumes and creates in its enactment, cultural features, and that these features can be understood, partly at least, as a metasocial commentary about identity, action itself, feelings, relations, and living in place, then part of this commentary has to do with doing the right thing, in the right way. In other words, when conversing, we do what we do, partly at least, because we think it is right, good, or somehow aesthetically pleasing to do so (see, e.g., Cameron, 1995, 2000). Ways of acting, being, relating, feeling, and dwelling are at any time possibly subjected to moral and aesthetic considerations, questioning whether that part is fitting to the conversational occasion. In this sense, conversation is normative or "hygienic" conduct in Deborah Cameron's sense, an enactment of, or accountable through claims of "legitimacy." These are always, to some degree, local claims. Although the symbolic aura of proper action is thus everpresent for the uptake in any conversation, the local means for doing so, and its meanings are indeed available for keeping the conversational car on the pathways of cultures.

Exploring a variety of cultural moves in conversation of course raises many questions and issues. Among them: What moves should be made next? What channels or instruments for communicating are being presumed, and valued, for now, at this point in the conversation? Is one, or should one, at this point, employ a nonverbal, and/or verbal means of expression? Through what forms? As we talk, who are the focal agents in the conversation? What social positions and relations are being presumed or forged? Is one (heard to be) speaking as a spokesperson or for one's self? Are there other, important communicative agents with us, in the blowing of the wind or the cawing of a crow? Across expressive systems, moves, channels and agents of communication are conceived differently, prioritized, used, and interpreted differently. This becomes especially clear in moments of intercultural contacts, as when one's verbally active response is heard not as pleasantness or friendliness but as suspicious, or another's silence is heard not as comforting but as disinterested. From ways of holding one's eyes and face, to ways of speaking, to ways of hearing nonhuman sounds, we differently produce and audit, thus differently conceive and utilize various instruments in conversation. Understanding how these different parts are differently crafted within expressive systems, what these parts are believed to be, and to be valued for, can help us understand the cultural status of various moves, channels, and sequences in conversation. It is to various explorations of these, and their cultural shaping, that we now turn.

ENDNOTES

1. The image I have in mind echoes one supplied by Harvey Sacks (1995) who explored "small parts of a thing" and built "out from them" (p. 159). The small parts I envision are also, at times, put into different cultural designs or "machines," thus the conversational gadgets and gismos are being used to build different models of conversation. See Hester and Eglin (1997), and also Emmanuel Schegloff (1995). See also the approach to discourse explicated in Ron and Suzanne Scollon's (1995) studies of intercultural communication.
2. The work builds on earlier works that explore cultural variability and intercultural encounters in the United States and various other nations, with a particular investigative stance being used to understand those as culturally infused, interactional accomplishments (Carbaugh, 1990a).
3. In 1986, Gerry Philipsen and I published a bibliography of well over 200 books and articles on the subject (Philipsen & Carbaugh, 1986). The introduction to the second edition of Richard Bauman's and Joel Sherzer's

(1990) book provides another important review. Surveys of related literatures are also available in Carbaugh (1995) and Philipsen (2002).

4. See the similar methodological stance discussed by J. Keith Chick (1996).

5. The order of problem raised here is, in John Searle's (1990) term, of the illocutionary force of an utterance. The response to the problem given below is a rendering of motivated actions, within sequences, and their focal themes via a culturally based expressive system, for which Searle's dimensions are indeed, at times, helpful.

⫷ 2 ⫸

Conversation as a Culturally Rich Phenomenon

People, as people, are doubtless much the same everywhere. That is what you commit yourself to in calling them people, rather than Egyptians, Buddhists, or speakers of Turkish. But the parts they play, the parts available for them to play, are not. (1995, p. 51)

—Clifford Geertz

With the beginning of a new century, we continue to experience the consequences and challenges of recent trends on human lives and relations.[1] One involves new technologies—of computer and travel—that at once decrease our senses of space and time, while increasing the masses of information available to us. A result of this trend is the challenge of putting all available information into some usable forms, making it something practical to some occasion of social life. A second trend revolves around population growth, group movements, and human migration. With this and the first trend comes an increase in contact among peoples and a dual awareness of one's distinctiveness and another's difference. How can and should one live with this distinctiveness and difference? A third trend is *globalization*, a new economic arena in which many jobs involving international travel and trade, with corporate viability, and national security deriving from worldwide cooperation. How can and should we live and work in this everpresent arena?

I begin with these trends in order to characterize movement in three directions: from an increase in technological and informational capability, to the attendant need to order and give form to that capability; from a larger and more mobile population, to the attendant need to recognize the depth of human distinctiveness within, and diversity among those various populations; and from an economic movement of integration, to the attendant need to recognize the wealth of tribal traditions that are activated in that very process. In summary, these technological, migratory, and economic trends carry weighty consequences, and attendant needs. One way of summarizing these trends is to draw attention to an urgent condition for satisfying all of these needs: the condition of giving each human culture, population, and tradition its due, while also exploring how each interacts with others. This, I think, is a, if not *the*, most prominent challenge of our age.

One set of responses to this challenge has been built around one kind of psychological model. From this view, characterizations are made of people as having a personality of a general type, and that type of personality is characterized along rather abstract dimensions. One recent conception has discussed this as "the collective programming of the mind which distinguishes the members of one category from another" (e.g., see Hofstede, 1980, quoted in Lewis, 2000, p. 25). Such thinking leads to generalizations such that Danes are more individualistic than the Taiwanese, or that the Italians are more authoritarian and hierarchical than the Swedes, or that Finns are more collectivist than people in the United States. The need to give form to diverse populations and traditions is met, from this view, with a kind of psychological diagnosis along abstract dimensions. Practical training that uses this general view leads thinking in the directions of a group's traits and its presumable, general dispositions. Proponents of this general view and of its practical uses are of course quick to caution against using this view too rigidly, and are, sometimes, quick to call for other ways of addressing the challenges just outlined.

Another set of starting points offers a complementary view. With it, we turn more to contexts of conversation, and less to personalities of peoples; more to interactional forms and styles, and less to psychological traits and dispositions; more to social and cultural situations, and less to abstract and universal dimensions.

From this view, the need to give form to diverse populations and traditions is met with a view to human conversations, with the diagnosis of these being less in terms of specieswide psychology and structure, and more in terms of culturally situated communication practices.

Beginning here helps us first to formulate a basic dynamic. We might ask: In giving conversational form to diversity, are we creating integration or division, are we uniting or separating? I want to respond generally by saying, in some situations we do one; in others, the other. Yet, in any one situation, both dimensions are active to some degree. Each, on occasion, can be advantageous; each can also be detrimental. Underlying dynamic movements of this kind are, I think, two sides of a universal coin, human want, or desire: the desire to be, at times, in some ways, like everyone else, yet also the desire to be different. In other words, on some occasions we want to be treated alike, as a member of a group. On others, we want our differences recognized. I think it is productive to think of these universal wants, less as psychological needs—although they are to some degree that, and more as a play and counterplay of contextual, interactional, and conversational dynamics. Casting the dynamic this way, as an interactional play between, or a possible balancing of these desires, we can begin to notice what we are saying—as culturally infused conversationalists—by focusing on the situated occasions in which we say to ourselves, and others, that we are in some ways alike yet we are also different.

In addressing this dynamic, we can bring conversations and cultures into a single view, and in so doing, amplify the need for a dual attentiveness to similarities and differences. There are, as always, attendant risks. As we emphasize the similarities among conversations and cultures, so we risk denying the differences; as we emphasize the differences, so we risk denying the similarities. Any attention to these matters must, therefore, remain cognizant of both, keeping in mind both the common humanity that is indeed evident, yet also, in some ways, the features that distinguish the one from the other.[2]

I return to these rather general matters later. To move our discussion a little closer to the ground, let me begin by describing three conversational scenes that derive from research projects that I have been conducting over the past years.[3] Each scene presented here is about social occasions in which different cultural agents are conversing with each other. Each describes an actual event. I describe each in an effort to introduce the general thesis that culture inhabits conversations, and to demonstrate the point that we can think about and practice such conversations better by taking this thesis quite seriously. As we move through these scenes and analyses, I hope to suggest both what such a view offers to people—like us—who are striving to give productive form to human diversity, as well as what these ideas might offer for building new, locally robust, world communities.

ENGLISH AND USAMERICAN CULTURES IN CONVERSATION

During the fall of 1993, I was in England, residing at the University of Oxford's Linacre College. Upon arriving there, I found that I was frequently a part of an interactional pattern that was somewhat puzzling to me, and I presume puzzling in different ways to my English acquaintances. I recorded several of these conversations in my field notes. My first entry of this kind follows:

While sitting in a pub in Oxford having lunch, a friendly gentleman in his mid 30s sat down beside me with his meal.

1. He said: Hello.
2. I replied: Hello.
3. He said: What brings you here?
4. I: I'm visiting Linacre College.
5. He said: Oh, yes, are you a student?
6. I: In a broad sense, yes (laughing) but I've come to join two research teams.
7. He: Oh, what are you studying?
8. I: One group is studying communication and identity. The other is studying environmental discourses.
9. He: Oh, yes, mighty interesting. Are you a member of the college?
10. I: (pause) I'm here at the invitation of Professor Harré.
11. (pause)
12. He: What is it that you study?
13. I: Cultural patterns of communication and intercultural encount ers.
14. He: Oh, you're an anthropologist?
15. I: No, not really, although my undergraduate degrees were in anthropology and communication, but what I study mostly are communication processes. In the United States we have academic departments whose primary purpose is to study communication.
16. He: (surprised) Oh, yes, uh-huh.

As we went on to our respective lunches, I believe we both had the sense that this exchange was less than fully satisfying. Although I eventually learned to work my way through encounters like this in a better, that is, more appropriately Oxford way, I had in this early exchange helped create somewhat of a mutually puzzling situation. Why might this be so? And can we find evidence in this encounter that different cultural orientations are involved?

The first four lines of the encounter seem to proceed rather unproblematically. If we look for a minute at the English gentleman's question on line 5, with his question he is searching for some way to position me, or place me, or identify me, within the social scheme of things that is, Oxford. Given my reply, that I was "in a broad sense" a student, and a member of "two research teams," it seemed quite probable to him that I was "a member of the college," thus his question on line 9. My pause and (to him) ambiguous response on line 10 about being here at someone's invitation, led him to try another way to find out about me, and thus to ask on line 12 about what I study. My short response about communication and cultural patterns led him, again, to supply a term familiar to him for such matters, on line 14, "an anthropologist," which I subsequently revised, supplying a rather longer identifier of my own on line 15. His response to this was a rather frustrated, conversation stopping, and less than satisfying, "Oh, yes, uh-huh."

The Oxford man had in so many words asked three common questions that typically allow questioners to identify participants in Oxford's England. Given that I was there and somehow affiliated with a part of the university, he presumed he could employ a prominent way of identifying me in this group as perhaps "a student," "a member of a college," or as one who is affiliated with an "academic department" or "unit." Affirmative responses to any one of these questions is richly coded, and deeply meaningful in Oxford's England. If one is a student or not, if one is a member of a college, and if so, of which college, this speaks volumes (especially about one's relative rank in the hierarchy of positions and prestige so prevalent there).

Responses to questions as these, as the questions themselves, then, if responsive in the local, English language, are culturally loaded, such that with these few words, one can become a known player in the social scene, positioned within the local social hierarchy, and thus, as such, an active participant in the interactional play that everyone native to Oxford knows as Oxford. At a more general level, questions as these, and the framing of responses to them in terms of social positions, statuses, differences between classes of people, and the arrangement of these into a social hierarchy are characteristic parts of many other English scenes, and conversations.[4]

Eventually, I came to understand some of this local style, and to formulate my responses to these questions in a way that was more immediately accessible, and more ably communicative to my English acquaintances. In short, I learned some lines of the English conversational script. But this of course begs the question of what I was doing in this earlier encounter. Eventually, retrospectively, I came to hear my remarks in these initial exchanges in this way: On line 4, 1 attempted (although somewhat inadequately in the local English code) to express an affiliation as a visitor to a college; on line 10, I tried to make my place known by stating a professional relationship with a prominent member of that college; and eventually on line 15, I tried to explain the academic discipline of my studies. What I was saying was this: I'm visiting a college, at the invitation of one of its members, and studying communication with others. This seemed, at the time, to be an adequate way of describing myself. But also, later, on reflection, I eventually realized that I was not mentioning other things that I could have mentioned, and that my English partners would have been relieved to hear, for example, that I had a social position, that "I was elected by college members to be a Visiting Senior Member of Linacre College." Mentioning this would have placed me in a role (as a Senior

Member) within a social hierarchy (in one of the graduate colleges) that was familiar to them, and thus they could have aligned their actions more easily with me.

Why, then, had I not mentioned this early on, my role within Oxford's social hierarchy? I think the reason is mainly a cultural one, and goes like this: This kind of identification, or reference—as a position within a social hierarchy—is less valued in some American scenes in which I had been socialized, because it foregrounds issues of social class, social differentiation, and stratification. Rather than these themes, I had been taught to prefer that one's personal interests and experiences be expressed, while minimizing social differences. To mention one's social positions is, then, in so many words, to re-create social class and hierarchy where some might prefer hearing, and speaking about personal matters and equitable themes. It's not that these features of some American discourse deny the existence of social class and hierarchy. It is that its display in conversation is at times devalued, rather than being a prominent theme for conversational display. The cumulative effect, here, are two cultures in conversation, one in terms of social positions and the other in terms of personality. I fear this is one more bit of evidence for George Bernard Shaw's humorous observation that "The Americans and the British are two people divided by the same language." Using the same language in fundamentally different ways is cause, I think, for many deep confusions, and reason, I think, for careful study of cultures in conversation.

RUSSIAN AND USAMERICAN CULTURES IN CONVERSATION

In the late 1980s, many Russians immigrated to the northeastern United States. Also at that time, international initiatives between Russia and the United States had led to an increase in cultural and educational exchanges (e.g., see Grimshaw, 1992). One such exchange involved the faculty of Russian and American business schools in discussions about their academic programs, with the explicit goal of helping the Russians learn the basic principles of free-market economics. In 1989, the business faculty at the University of Massachusetts eagerly awaited a visiting group of Russian professors. After the Russians arrived on campus, an initial meeting was called between the two groups, with a tone of informality, the spirit being to meet each other, gather information about each other's academic programs, and thus find out how each might be helpful to the other. The meeting occurred in a university seminar room and transpired in this way.

A representative of each group helped introduce the participants to each other. Titles and last names were used, for example, "Professor Smith, this is Professor Mishkutov," thus saying something about the relative equal statuses of all involved. After the introductions, the Russian and American participants began exchanging information about their respective programs of business and management, describing the resources, curriculum, faculty and so on, of each. This went very smoothly, until a rather prolonged period of escalated boasts about each program gave way to other conversational moves.

The Americans at the meeting began wondering out loud about what the Russians wanted to learn about American business schools. One American faculty member said, "How could we be of help to you?" And, "What would you like to know about our school?" The Russian professors perhaps taking this to be all too pushy and premature, and as perhaps a request for information that could divulge shortcomings, responded by describing further how well their business schools were operating, and by detailing the accomplishments of their colleagues and research staff. As one Russian professor put it, in an impassioned tone, "We have a very good, very good school. Our staff has published numerous books and articles!" then went on in detail to describe a variety of impressive academic achievements. The Americans found this to be rather pompous and irrelevant.

As a result of this dynamic, the Americans did not discover what the Russians wanted or needed to know from them, which was—it seemed to the Americans—the main stated reason for their trip to the United States. Thus, the Americans' desire to be helpful to the Russians was frustrated (although they did hear that the Russian school had some major accomplishments). Feeling the meeting needed to be "loosened up a bit," the Americans began disclosing some of the problems they experienced with their American school and bureaucracy. Details were being given by the Americans about "bureaucratic blunders," projects being underfunded, and too few staff for the work that needed to get done, and so on. This tactic was adopted by the Americans in the hope that it would liberate the Russians from the famous "showy" Russian front and that the Russians would in turn, likewise, describe some of the difficulties they had had in their Russian schools.[5] The Russians, however, found this tactic rather unusual, quite puzzling, and perhaps lacking any virtue whatsoever. The convener sensed the meeting, at this point, was quite strained and at cross-purposes, and would best be adjourned.

What had transpired in this group's conversation? And can we unravel some of its mystery by reflecting on the cultural forms in it? In the middle stage of this intercultural encounter, the Americans invoked one of their conversational rules: When with outsiders, and one needs information, one should ask rather directly for it. In turn, if one is asked for information, one should be forthcoming with it, especially if it implies a problem, for talk with others about problems is one means

of addressing and solving those very problems. This is a kind of efficiency rule for acting in public, erected on political and cultural bases
of "free speech," and seeks to foreground facts, problems, and
possible solutions.

The Russian business professors, however, invoked at the same
time a rule of their own: When with outsiders, and one is asked about
one's "motherland" (as Russians call Russia), or one of its institutions,
one should espouse its virtues. This is a kind of face rule for presenting
one's identity by foregrounding the collective virtues of one's nation
and its people. The rule is erected on shared moral premises, collective virtues, and foregrounds images of the good (rather than
statements of fact).

When the American professors were not getting the information they
sought, they presumed that talking about their problems would lead,
in turn, to the Russians talking about theirs. Although this is a common way to talk in many American public scenes, it places talk about
factual problems over that about virtues and, as such, violates a Russian preference for such conduct in Russian occasions.

The general dynamic that resulted from these different rules is rather
ironic: As Americans discussed their problems with American business
schools, they discussed what the Russians least needed (and wanted) to
know. The Russians of course wanted to know the strengths and accomplishments in order to adapt them to their own circumstances. On the
other hand, as the Russians discussed the virtues and accomplishments of their business school, they discussed what the Americans least
needed (and wanted) to know. The Americans wanted to know its shortcomings so they could be helpful in making the school better.

These basic rules for public discussion with outsiders and the different conversational themes they foreground (the American foregrounding of facts over virtues, and the Russian foregrounding of
virtues over facts) are observable in any number of situations.[6]

Since making these observations a few years ago, I have heard several Russian speakers in public who were asked questions of fact yet
responded with impassioned, even artful expressions of an image of
the good, presenting a moral tale of an ideal world as it should be. Russians have likewise heard many Americans stating—sometimes in
great detail—troubling truths, rather than expressing common virtues
or the shared fiber of a strong moral life. In fact, as a result in part of
conversing in these distinctive cultural ways, Russians are often led to
portray Americans as soul-less or immoral, too willing to spill the dis-
creditable truth and unable to state any shared morality; Americans in
turn are often led to portray Russians as not fully reasonable, as unable to answer basic questions of fact, too willing in public to be impassioned, too righteous, to the point of being illogical. Given this general

difference in cultural rules for conversation, one wonders to what degree the Russian ultranationalist Mr. Zhirinovsky's public comments—such as the stated desire to reannex Finland—are designed as facts of policy, and to what degree they are more aptly heard as bids to passionately reassert an image of a strong Russia. Evidence suggests the latter dimension may be operating, but also can be a source of deep trouble, and can be deeply perplexing to those who express facts and morals quite differently.

FINNISH AND USAMERICAN CULTURES
IN CONVERSATION

Since 1992, I have had the tremendous privilege of traveling and talking to many audiences in Finland. In 1993, when I was giving a series of such talks, I heard a story repeatedly, told as many stories are, as if it was true. Typically, this story was told after my talk, when a small gathering of people would be discussing the general occasion. Because the story was told in my presence, and because it was told repeatedly after typical comments were made about Finns' shyness and reserve, I think its main point was to characterize differences in communicative styles between Finns—especially Hamé Finns, from the central region of Finland—and Americans, albeit in a rather humorous way. As we were seated at a dining table in a university cafeteria, enjoying our "pulla" (sweet bread) and after a colleague expressed some surprise at the quantity of discussion that followed the lecture, a second Finnish colleague told the story this way:

> An American academic visited here just last year from [insert any American] University. He gave an hour-long lecture about social science [insert your topic], then paused for discussion. He must have waited a whole 5 seconds! [said sarcastically]. After no discussion was produced by us (the audience), he began chiding the audience, and after that didn't produce any discussion, he got angry and started calling us names!! He embarrassed himself and all of us, and they quickly adjourned the meeting. [Laughter].

This brief story apparently says something to Finns about Americans through the character of the professor. On the face of it, it suggests that at least this American, and perhaps others too, can speak at great length (about an hour), in a way that is sometimes impatient (waits only 5 seconds), sometimes demanding (expects much of their audience), and sometimes insulting (insensitive to audience customs, calling them names). The story also, in its turn, and by implication, says some things about Finnish communication. Those who hear the story are invited to think of a Finnish interactional style, relative to an American one, as being more properly reserved, or sometimes as even highly patient, or thoughtful (as one Finn said, "We take the time we need to formulate a remark we think is worthy, rather than make a merely impulsive reaction"). The story also suggests that the Finnish style demands less from large numbers of participants (as another Finn said, "We talk, and expect talk, only if there is something really important to say"). Further, the story suggests Finns are careful to say things properly, and not contentiously (as a third Finn said, "We would never be so rude or confrontational to others"). In sum, the story portrays an American through a style that is talkative, impatient, and demanding, while implicitly contrasting that style with a Finnish one that is more reserved, respectful, and deferential.

Although this interpretation of the messages in the story says quite a bit, I believe there is more to the story than this. There is displayed in it a contrast in some basic rules for social conversation, and associated with them are presumptions from two different cultural worlds, which we discuss further in a subsequent chapter. These rules are perhaps distinctively Hamé Finnish burdens to place on conversation, for if conversation is to be produced accordingly, it requires a careful, studied thoughtfulness and considerable reflection—quintessential qualities of Finnishness (in Finnish, *mietiskella*).

Preferences or rules like these, I think, perhaps tell us something of the self-avowed "reserve" (or *pitaa*) that Finnish speakers at times are said to profess, and possess. These cultural premises for conversation may help explain a self-avowed Finnish lack of, or distaste for small talk. Such cultural features help us understand why some Finns seldom use personal names in conversation, for, as a Finnish friend put it to me, smiling: "Why use names? If you don't know each other it's presumptuous. And if you know each other, it's all so damn obvious." Further, applying these cultural standards for conversation may require prolonged, and perhaps even profound periods of silence. It takes time to formulate remarks that are carefully thought about, properly presented, and adequately reflected on. In a country where commonality of lifestyle and belief is not only presumed, but often actualized, social living can be conducted accordingly, with conversation searching to go beyond the all-too-common surface of social life.

The Finnish story also includes another character, an American. It is notable that Americans can so easily violate these Finnish preferences for conversation. In other words, not only the nature of an utterance (as studied and thoughtful), but its placement in the ongoing flow of social life is cultural. USAmerican speakers can speak quickly about things that are personally involving to them, more than weighing the social worthiness of their thoughts; or they may say things not very important to them—perhaps in the role of "the devil's advocate"—in the spirit of prodding others to speak, and to hear what they have to say. This peculiarly American character can speak a lot, about almost anything, but seems especially fond of the "self." The cultural preferences or rules for this kind of American conversation revolve around the belief that one can and should speak, one can and should speak about the self, its history, experiences, and opinions; and that one should not let others inhibit the willingness to speak in public. The main theme and warrant for these actions are not so much the social or moral worthiness of a contribution to conversation, as it is the importance of the contribution to the speaker. In a country where everyone is presumably different, on personal and other levels, it is incumbent on each to say what they have to say, so that some common life can be woven out of these threads of difference. Unlike Finland where a relatively deeper common fabric can be presumed and conversation seeks to move beyond it, for the American system to work, differences are often presumed and commonality must be somehow built or demonstrated out of them. Put simply, Finnish conversation can at times presume commonality and must seek beyond that for its creativity and diversity, whereas American conversation can presume some diversity and must build commonality out of it.[7]

This deeper reading of the story may help us understand not only the incident between the American professor and the Finnish audience, but also the importance of the stories Finns tell about Americans, Americans tell about Finns, indeed, that each "one tells of an other." By attending to such stories, of conversations and cultures, we can understand generally what happens whenever we act together and tell stories about each other. It is not so much then, on the order of a psychological diagnosis that Finns are reserved, or that Americans are talkative, or that Russians foreground virtues over facts, or that the British are status or class conscious. It is more that each may, at times, converse in characteristic forms or styles through discourses and codes that are situated in a scene, and are distinctive to it. Each also, on occasion, gets caught up with others.

How, then, given these particular and general dynamics, can we understand cultures in conversations? Can we offer others—through our education and training—anything from this view? What can we suggest about living, with these forms of knowledge, amidst the diverse human customs and traditions in our contemporary worlds? I conclude by sketching some ingredients and prospects that underlie these stories and the view that created them.

First, it can be fruitful and gratifying to focus on one basic goal: To help people decipher the puzzles of contexts, and more specifically to help them reflect on the promise and perplexities of culturally infused conversations. How can we help people become reflective investigators, and critical users of cultures in conversations?

One set of ingredients I have already introduced and applied. These are the efforts to help keep people focused on interactional events, rather than on personalities or psyches; focused on contexts, rather than on psychological traits; and on cultural features, forms, and meanings, rather than on abstract dimensions or diagnoses. These ingredients, when applied, can lead us to knowledge about conversations, in contexts, and their cultural meanings. In my earlier remarks, they produced reflections on English and American encounters in an Oxford pub; Russian and American encounters about business; and Finnish and American encounters concerning proper conduct with others. Together, the ingredients help ground our knowledge, of ourselves and others, in actual moments of living together. What the ingredients work against are easy attributions of traits to ourselves and other group members, for we all know that any member of any group may or may not act accordingly. If we think on the basis of conversations in context, we look and listen first for particular features and forms of conversation that may be distinctive in a scene or community, and if examined, we can notice its distinctive preferences, rules, terms, and meanings. As the variety of conversations—that is, life—occurs, our reflections are thus guided accordingly. It is this attentiveness to conversation and with it, its cultural coding, and its reflective practice, that I believe holds considerable promise in our research and teaching.

I have mentioned the ingredients of conversation, contexts, and culture. I should amplify the cultural ingredient a bit further. What this ingredient suggests is simply this: Conversations—through deep premises, targeted themes, preferences, and styles—speak beyond themselves and, as such, include a rich metasocial commentary about people, relations, actions, feelings, and living in places. Conversations derive from a history of practices, and can subsequently re-create or transform those very practices. For this reason, we can explore how an encounter in a pub says one thing about being English, and something else about being American; how meetings among business leaders say one thing about being Russian, another about being American, and so on. Each such conversation brings to it, and uses, orientations to living, different beliefs and values about being and relating, about acting, about feeling, about dwelling in places. Monitoring and explicating these helps unveil the basic cultural dimensions in conversations. Understanding how they infuse conversation with culture will help us respond to the challenges before us, to act and reflect, to research and teach, accordingly.

Another dynamic reminds us that cultures infuse conversation within a kind of dialectical process. For example, immanent in some intercultural episodes is a synthesis of differences or of "horizons" (to borrow Gadamer's (1997) phrase). As a Finnish and a German style, or an East Asian and American style are creatively melded—each to the other—in the course of doing business, a fusing of differences can occur (see Hastings, 2001). Immanent in other episodes, perhaps on occasion among some Russian and American business professors, is division, differences being presumed and reasserted, thus creating a continued fission between the ways of each. One dynamic is thus captured as communal conversations contact one another, with—at one end—each creatively synthesizing, or—at the other—each reasserting itself against (or over) the other.

A similar dynamic operates in this grand conversational process, and plays on the dialectic between the global and the local. Whether the cultures animating conversations are widely prominent such as popular Western mediated culture, or are in the midst of being made such as Eurowide culture, some such macrosenses of self and place are immanent on some occasions among people. Whatever these are—whether deemed mediated American, Asian, European, or African—if they are active, they inhabit those situated scenes in which we practice social life, ways of living that are radically of a place, and thus are more sensitive to the nuances of the people in that place. In fact, some fundamental lessons concerning environmental, economic, and political living are now being learned by paying careful attention to local conversations (principal among these being from indigenous cultures). I think it best, therefore, that we begin by recasting our thinking about contemporary worlds, less on the model of one global village, and more on the level of thousands of interdependent local cultures, working (and sometimes fighting) together, creating within and between them various communities of social life.

To know cultures in conversation fully, then, if this is at all possible, is to know these processes of integration and division, between global and local dynamics. This knowledge will come slowly and will involve commitments of time, education in local cultures, histories, and careful attention to the communal conversations that give them form. If we incorporate these learnings into our studies, we might be able to create one kind of knowledge that is lacking in the contemporary world. In the process, we will help by providing one potent way of giving form to its diverse customs and traditions of living.

Focusing on intercultural encounters this way can help build powerful communal myths with many possible implications, from integration to division, globally to locally, through many necessary codes, from British social classes to Russian souls to Finnish quietude to American selves to indigenous peoples' natured ways. Constructing communities through scenes of cultures in conversation is to model communities around multiple hubs of activity, with no center being mandated. Distinctive cultural customs can thus be acknowledged as part of the process, and brought into the play of a community's conversation, one with the others, each holding a place, or a voice, along with (or even against) the others.

Each way of conversing, in turn, for the account to include productive and reflective interaction, as the pragmatist Josiah Royce (1908) reminded us at the turn of the last century, must actively seek others' ways as a source of possible enrichment for our own. In our contemporary worlds, this is no longer an option, but an obligation.

The myths that will sustain us in our lives together will only come out of a community where we tell and listen not only to our own, but also to other's stories and scenes. This, again, provides one way of responding to the technological, migratory and economic trends of our age, and to the associated problems of masses of information and international battles. The response suggests that we give form at the boundaries, where diverse human populations come together. In the process, as we hear cultures in conversation, and help others to so hear their own and others' codes, we must be willing to hear plot lines that are sometimes rewarding, others that are warring. What we say to ourselves about ourselves and others must ably capture the breadth of truths about living, and the various scenes that constitute troubled places. Of course, we must also give scrutable voice to the peaceful places and times when the conversations are mutually gratifying. As we monitor cultures in conversation, we can give forms to the diversity of places and peoples, and their ways of living together. In the process, we create a vision of interdependence, with each inextricably bound to an other, or others. Similarly, as we struggle to respond to the technological, migratory, and economic trends of our age, we not only can, but must form newer versions of our worlds as they are, versions that take conversations, contexts, and cultures as their starting points. As a result, better visions will be created, with each erected around the declaration of interdependence that is, a way of living together, today. By giving form to the diverse communities and traditions in the world, in this way, with our sense tuned to cultures and conversations, we will have more productive scenes to live, and better stories to tell.

ENDNOTES

1. This is a slightly revised version of a keynote lecture given at the conference of SIETAR Europa, University of Jyvaskyla, Finland, March 12,1994. I thank Liisa Salo-Lee and David Marsh of the University of Jyvaskyla for the invitation to participate in the conference and Leslie McBee of the America Center in Helsinki for making my participation in the conference possible. An earlier version of the essay was published

in the conference proceedings under the title: "Cultures in Conversation: Prospects for New World Communities" (see Carbaugh, 1994b).

2. The dynamic introduced here derives from Kenneth Burke (1965), is central to Philipsen (1987), and explored in earlier studies (Carbaugh, 1988/1989, 1996b, pp. 123–139, 157–202; and Wick, 1998).

3. Each will be presented in greater detail in the subsequent chapters of this book. Each of the three stories told here are part of larger research projects that I have been conducting over the past several years. Each derives from a larger scholarly "narrative" that is not narrated in this essay, but is nonetheless a condition of its production. The general theoretical and methodological commitments of the approach are explicated elsewhere (see Carbaugh, 1990a&c; Carbaugh & Hastings, 1992). The following stories derive most explicitly from several more detailed studies that explore the cultural communication of Russians (e.g., Carbaugh, 1993c), Americans (e.g., Carbaugh, 1988b), Finns (e.g., Carbaugh, 1994) and an indigenous American people (e.g., Carbaugh, 1993b).

4. A recent study of West German interactional forms by Stephen Kalberg (1987) indicated that there are some similarities (and differences) between it and the British one sketched here.

5. I borrow the idea of a "showy" front from the Russian scholar, Anna Pavlovskaya, who says, based on her historical research that "Russians are inclined to show-off, especially when dealing with outsiders" (see Pavlovskaya, 1994).

6. This general dynamic has been evident in many intercultural contacts between Russians and Americans, including intercultural encounters on televised talk shows and beauty pageants (see Carbaugh, 1993a). See further the transcript in Grimshaw (1992).

7. Interested readers may want to consult several studies of Finnish communication (e.g., Sallinen- Kuparinen, 1986, Lehtonen & Sajavaara, 1985; Mauranen, 1993).

⚜ 3 ⚜

Silence, and Third-Party Introductions:
An American and Finnish Dialogue
(with Saila Poutiainen)[1]

University of Helsinki, Finland

Several winters ago, I (DC) was living with my family as foreigners in Finland, where I was teaching and doing research. As a recipient of a Fulbright Grant, I had been asked to participate in activities at two universities. I had been anticipating an initial trip to the second Finnish university, the University of Suomi, for a couple of weeks.[2] After settling in at our Finnish home, I was excited about traveling to Suomi, where I would meet the Finnish colleagues with whom I would be working periodically over the next several months.

On arriving there, I marveled at the modern facilities and the advanced technologies available in classrooms and computer rooms. I also felt energized by the natural landscape, with the main part of the university being located on a hill with nice views through pines onto a large lake. It was a beautiful winter day, with a deep blue sky above a snow covered ground. I felt energized and was ready to go!

But I was not ready for what happened next. On meeting my Finnish host, Professor Silvo, we began walking through the building where my office would be located. As we moved down a hallway of office suites, I noticed that some people—on seeing us—seemed to be avoiding us by moving quickly into their offices. After this happened a couple of times, I asked my host if I might be able to meet my future colleagues, especially Professor Virtanen. I knew we shared some interests in our studies and thought that perhaps I had seen him out of the corner of my eye, going into an office. Professor Silvo replied that we could meet him later, perhaps on my next visit in a couple of weeks.

Given my customary ways, these introductory events seemed puzzling and cumbersome. I wondered to myself, "Why can't Professor Virtanen at least say 'Hi'?" And "Why aren't the others here more forthcoming with their greetings?" I was accustomed to meeting people quickly, with perhaps a "Hello" and a quick exchange of smiles, names, and pleasantries. But nothing of the sort was happening here on my first trip to Suomi. I was puzzled. Moreover, on meeting someone, the exchanges seemed, at least to me at times, quite cumbersome. I had heard and read about "the silent Finn" and was not sure when I should step into a conversation. Moreover, when I did so, I was not sure what to say, how long I should speak, nor what obligations I had to open or close the conversation.

What follows is a record of one such meeting that occurred on this, my first trip to Suomi. The meeting involved me with a group of colleagues that I had only met on this day, but whom eventually, over the years, have become friends. The introductory event, on this occasion, involved a Finnish university administrator, two Finnish faculty members, and me. In particular, the event involved me in my role as an American Fulbright Professor who was to meet an important Finnish university administrator (Professor Jussi Virtanen, male). More specifically, in this exchange, I am being introduced to the administrator by a Finnish professor (Anna Silvo, female). We are being accompanied by another Finnish professor (Jussi Levo, male). The event begins as the two Finnish professors escort me down a university corridor to meet the administrator, Jussi Virtanen. He is visible through a slightly opened door.[3] This is what happened:

1. Anna Silvo knocks on the door.

2. Jussi Virtanen: *Jaa*. [Yes].

3. Silvo: *Hei, anteeks, voinko mä esitellä sulle meidän uuden Fulbright professorin?* [Hi, excuse me, could I introduce to you our new Fulbright Professor?].

4. Virtanen: *Joo*. [Okay.] (Virtanen rises from his desk, walks around in front of it so he is facing Silvo on his right, Carbaugh in front of him, and Levo on his left.)

5. Silvo: Jussi, I would like you to meet Dr. Carbaugh.
   And (Silvo looks at Carbaugh while gesturing to Virtanen) Professor Virtanen.

6. Virtanen: Hello. (Shaking hands with Carbaugh).

7. Carbaugh: Good to meet you.

8. (10 to 16 second pause)

9. Virtanen: So, uhm, when did you arrive?

10. Carbaugh: Well, we arrived in early January and we've been here for about a month now.

11. And it's been very good to be here. We've been able to see just a little bit of Finland but

12. what we've seen we like very much. We feel like we're at home. With the good help of

13. people like Anna and Jussi, they've made us feel even more at home.

14. (12 to 20 second pause)

15. Virtanen: Have you been meeting people here?

16. Carbaugh: Well, yes, uh, we met several people this morning and uh I've heard a little bit

17. about their research projects and that's been very interesting. It sounds like there are

18. many interesting things going on here. And uh I'm just so impressed with your physical

19. facilities. The buildings are so nice and your lab seems very well equipped.

20. (10 to 16.9 second pause)

21. Virtanen: So what are you going to do while you are here?

22. Carbaugh: Well uh mainly I have teaching obligations at another university. I have a

23. couple of lecture series. And then here at Suomi I'll be teaching and doing some

24. seminar work. And so most of my time will be spent teaching here and there.

25. (10 to 13.5 second pause)

26. Carbaugh: Well, it's been very good to meet you and I look forward to spending time at your university.

27. Virtanen shakes hands with Carbaugh, nods, smiles, and bows slightly. Silvo, Levo, and Carbaugh turn and leave.

As this event began, I felt rather comfortable, up through line 7 at least. However, at this point, as this event unfolded, I met what was for me a pause in the conversation that went well beyond what I anticipated in its place. As the seconds ticked by, and as is typical when sensing something may have gone awry, alarms began to sound in my mind. Perhaps I had done something wrong, or perhaps I was supposed to be doing something different, or saying something else. Why was this pause lasting so long? Finally, and thankfully from my view, Professor Virtanen broke the silence and asked me when I had arrived. I told him when we arrived, how things were going, and tried to indicate that Anna and Jussi had been fine hosts to me. I tried to offer some information that he could take up, ask me about, or build on. After doing this, however, there was no uptake on the matters I had mentioned, but again, an even longer pause! Perhaps up to 20 seconds long! What was going on? Had I done something wrong? My collar began to moisten as I looked to Jussi and Anna for nonverbal cues about what to do next. Both were delightfully calm, small smiles at the corner of their mouths. Were they smiling at me? All nonverbal indications from them seemed positive and good. Evidently, from their view, things were proceeding quite well, thank you! At the time, I found this hard to believe, especially when the next question from Professor Virtanen did not seem to relate to anything I had said earlier, but initiated another topic altogether, about the people I had been meeting.

And so the event went. As we cycled through the question–answer–silence sequence another time, it occurred to me that perhaps it was my responsibility to conclude our meeting. After all, I thought—perhaps unwittingly initiating an escape from the conversation—I may be taking too much of the administrator's valuable time. So, eventually, after the fourth and shortest of the pauses, I broke in with a closing, thanking Professor Virtanen for meeting me and indicating an interest in seeing him again.

Weeks after this exchange, I was having lunch with Professor Silvo. We were discussing a student project about uses of silence when the aforementioned exchange came to mind. I asked her about it and she said, yes, the use of long pauses in conversation—at least longer "when compared to the ones you Americans tend to do"—is common in Finnish conversation. But also, she said, these pauses are especially long when conversing with Professor Virtanen, even by Finnish standards! After discussing this for awhile, I asked her a question to which I thought I already knew the answer. "Should I have waited for Professor Virtanen to close the conversation?" She smiled kindly, said again how long his pauses tended to be. "You know," she said, "he's very Finnish." Then she answered my question: "Yes, it is up to him to close the conversation. He wanted to give the proper amount of time to meeting you." As a Finnish reader of this essay commented, "When meeting someone, we want to make sure there is enough time to really talk about something." I had not known enough to give Professor Virtanen, and this event, its "proper amount of time."[4]

We have provided some initial reactions to this event as they were formed, early on, by the American in it (DC). Now, let us add some additional reflections about this same event from a Finnish view. How might the conduct of this event, and initial reactions to it, be formulated from a Finnish participant?

When I (SP) look at this exchange, I cannot help but hear some common and important features of Finnish communication. According to my experience, these features are present and active in many intercultural communication situations, like this one. For example, consider Professor Silvo's response to DC about pauses in Finland being longer "when compared to the ones you Americans tend to do." Professor Silvo's comment here reflects her own considerable intercultural experiences, including living in the United States for several years. Clearly, she knew firsthand how Finnish and American pauses may differ in length. Perhaps more generally, such comments reflect the strong sense Finns can have about their way of communicating and how it contrasts with others' ways, such as American, German, and Japanese. For various reasons, Finns are interested in knowing what others think about Finns and Finnish communication. The images Finnish people have about themselves, relative to others, are partly based on images of others they have contacted personally or, especially for the younger generation, perhaps seen in Finnish popular culture and television. (Many popular American television programs are shown daily on Finnish television thus providing a daily contrast between this mediated "American" world and the Finnish one.) Based largely on these images, some Finns—especially those who have not traveled to the United States—may believe they "know" how Americans communicate, how they talk, and what they sound like. Thus, Finns may know that their pauses are at times much longer than those typical in some "American" scenes. When understanding this kind of intercultural encounter from the Finnish perspective, I believe it is important to remember this: One's prior personal contacts, experiences, and exposure to mediated images may establish expectations about others' communication, for example of Finns as being relatively silent or of Americans as being more talkative, with those expectations perhaps shaping parts of this kind of encounter.

A second important point to stress is the perceived language skills of the Finnish speakers. Although often in situations of speaking a foreign language with cultural others, and in spite of an obvious fluency with a foreign language, Finnish speakers may lack confidence or assurance in using that foreign language.[5] In our quoted scenario, English is required of the Finnish speakers, and this may be the second, third, or even the fourth language of a Finnish speaker.[6] Recall, in this scene, that Virtanen has to speak English not only with a respected native English speaker (DC), but also in the presence of two of his co-workers who are important to him.

To focus on the kind of hallway interaction just described, one event that may be getting done when DC first visited Finnish universities might be called, from the Finnish perspective, "getting to know, or getting acquainted with the workplace or house" (i.e., *tutustua taloon*). When one is doing, "getting acquainted with the workplace," a main initial activity involves walking around and seeing the facilities, the important offices, and hearing from the host about the workplace, its history, people, relationships, and the preferred daily procedures. Perhaps Silvo and Levo, and other faculty, were doing activities that are deemed appropriate to that kind of Finnish activity, that is, to helping DC "get acquainted with the department, workplace, or house." Such an activity, in Finland, doesn't necessarily involve verbal introductions with the people working in that department. The main activities in this Finnish activity of "getting acquainted with the house" would involve seeing the facilities and hearing about the workplace from a host or hostess. Naturally, of course, one might see people during such a visit, but here's an important point: In Finland, during this *tutustua taloon* activity among Finns, there would be no felt obligation to talk with visitors nor to be verbally introduced to them. A nod, a slight smile, and/or a "Hello" if passing them in the hallway would be quite enough, if that was even needed. "Getting acquainted with the workplace," that is, in this Finnish way, may require very little by way of verbal interaction with those one sees beyond the host. Minimizing verbal interaction can also be a way of not wasting DC's and other participants' time in relatively "superficial" matters, or in what some Finnish speakers call "unnecessary talk."

On this first visit, the host, Silvo, mentioned to DC that it may be best to meet some of her colleagues, including Professor Virtanen, after this first visit, at a later date. Indeed, Finnish viewers and readers of the introduction episode have called this event a "handshaking delegation" that can seem very distant and formal. Perhaps this is because of several reasons. Formal introductions are not part of the normal, daily professional communication in this Finnish scene, nor typically a part of initial visits. Formal introductions often require special preparation. As contrasted with a Finnish greeting such as an exchange of nods, a formal meeting may, perhaps even should, involve exchanging significant information and ideas. To get to know someone, or to meet someone formally, takes more time and is usually done directly and concisely by discussing one's official affairs, business, and duties. Professor Virtanen may have wanted the time to prepare for his first meeting with Professor Carbaugh, a highly respected guest, and perhaps Professor Virtanen wanted to make sure that the first meeting would be rewarding and productive for both Professor Carbaugh and himself. That kind of Finnish interaction might involve the Finnish style of "asia-talk," or "matter-of-fact" speaking. This style, prevalent in scenes of education, consists not so much of small talk and pleasantries but of substantial exchanges of important information on a variety of matters or topics. As such, asia-talk involves preparation in order to engage in direct, concise, and substantial discussion about one's official affairs, business, and duties that are worthy of the occasion.[7]

Notice then, from a Finnish view on these matters, several features of this conversation: Finnish interactions of this kind can presume something about American speaking based on the ways Americans have acted in the past, including images seen in Finnish popular culture. As a result, in scenes like the one already introduced, Americans may be relied on—by Finns—to talk a lot. Finns, on the other hand, especially when speaking a foreign language like English, may prefer to speak very little. The reliance on nonverbal conduct is readily intelligible to Finns, as in the folk event "getting acquainted with the workplace." In this event, only the assigned host is required to entertain the guest verbally. Moreover, Finnish events like these—the third party introduction and getting acquainted—do not necessarily incur the obligation from others of verbal communication with the guest. As a result, workers may move into offices quite appropriately without speaking to a visitor. Similarly, when being introduced to a visitor in Finland, only very little information needs to be exchanged verbally. If one is involved in such a formal meeting, this typically takes place in a small group and at a specified date and time. Further, both third-party introductions and getting acquainted rituals may be conducted through a folk style of asia-talk, which is rather straightforward, direct, and matter of fact about official affairs and duties. Note how this is quite unlike an American form known as "small talk," which may involve lengthy verbal exchanges of pleasantries.

Being mindful of these few Finnish cultural features, then, a participant might monitor the presented encounter somewhat differently than we did initially. Perhaps the Finnish communication, here, moves between actions one does when "getting acquainted with the workplace," and a more formal and meaningful meeting through the matter of fact, *asiallinen* style. With it, participants may anticipate a direct style of speaking, exchange information matter of factly, and interpret ideas accordingly. Understanding our exchange on the basis of these Finnish premises, suggests these further specific insights about it.

After Silvo introduced DC and Virtanen to each other (on line 5 through line 7), Virtanen asked DC about his time of arrival (line 9). DC's response to that question occurs on line 10, "We arrived in early January," but is followed by several more utterances about Finland, his feelings, and friends. Note how that same pattern is repeated as Virtanen asked his second question (on line 15): "Have you been meeting people here?" DC's answer is on line 16, "We met several people this morning," but again is followed by additional descriptive commentary about research projects, physical facilities, and laboratories. From a Finnish perspective, especially one accustomed to a kind of asia-talk that is concise and direct, DC has given a sufficient answer on line 9, and again on line 16. In those lines, from a Finnish view, he has already satisfactorily answered the questions. Such answers, like these, are what might be preferred as asia-talk, something short, matter of fact, and directly responsive to the queries. No more speaking is really required than this. As a result, the rest of DC's responses, although descriptive—and perhaps produced in a spirit of American small talk or exchanging pleasantries—may not be that significant, at least to Finns. A Finnish listener might even wonder: Why are these details forthcoming from DC? In fact, a Finn might, indeed, ask silently: What is he talking about? Isn't DC saying something else than what Virtanen asked of him? For example, when DC says on line 12, "We feel like we're at home," or on line 13, "Anna and Jussi, they've made us feel even more at home," a Finnish listener might wonder if DC is indeed telling the truth and being honest. Having said so much in this way, DC may easily be heard, like those Americans seen on TV, as so very American, talkative, even exaggerating a bit, and perhaps as being stereotypically superficial ("Can he really feel at home, as he says?"). Is he speaking the truth or just being nice? From a Finnish view, especially one mindful of talking *asia*, he may easily be heard as saying more than was required in this situation and be deemed guilty of stretching the truth a bit.[8]

Focusing for a moment on the Finnish pauses that are active in this exchange, we might ask why they are so long—at least when compared to the ones Americans might expect in their place. As already mentioned, one reason is this: Professor Virtanen is known for using long pauses, even longer than are typical by Finnish standards. More generally, pauses can be much longer in Finnish than in American communication. There are several reasons for this. First, it is customary for Finnish conversations to be punctuated by lengthy pauses, even if they are not as long as the ones in use here. Second, the long pauses might result from the Finnish speaker's speaking a foreign language, thus taking considerable time in order both to interpret the English being spoken and to formulate the proper responses in English. Third, introducing a foreigner (DC, in this scene) is to create a scene that is perhaps a bit unusual to some Finnish participants. The foreigner may do something unusual, like the expressive small-talk behavior, when the Finns might be preferring or expecting a more short, matter of fact asia-talk. As a result, expectations must be adjusted, and this takes time. Fourth, the occasion itself is to be respected and long pauses are a way of signifying it as such. Together, then, these features of the conversation lay some possible cultural ground for such long pauses in this situation.

What we have tried to do in our discussion is to notice features in one communication encounter that are deeply cultural. An American may notice people engaged in a practice who are, from his view, not talking very much, not trying to avoid long pauses, and when speaking, saying so little. Perhaps unwittingly, the American produces an American folk version of communication, small talk, and in so doing, does not quite meet the expectations of the occasion the Finnish participants have established. On the basis of these conversational features, a Finn may notice an American who, as expected, likes to talk a lot. Ready for verbal action, he says more than the occasion seems to warrant; he also says things other than expected, bringing informal affairs to a more formal occasion. Perhaps unwittingly, Finns may produce folk versions of communication including a Finnish form of "getting acquainted with a workplace" and "talking about matters of fact." To summarize with a metaphor, the encounter involves two scripts for the same play, two sets of lines for the same conversational scene, and thus results in a the "staging" of an improvised, intercultural drama.

We have come to understand the encounter, and similar others, through American and Finnish cultural features that are active when a foreigner in Finland is being introduced by a third party. Introductory encounters, as this, can provide a kind of dialogic drama between cultural discourses. As such, we note the preparation and propriety that may be preferred for a Finnish version, as Professor Silvo said about Professor Virtanen: "He wanted to give the proper amount of time to meeting you." A proper, formal meeting, from the vantage point of this script, requires time and adequate preparation. When this scene was discussed with other Finns, they produced these comments: "The whole scene certainly sounds very familiar! Slow pace, pauses, direct questions"; it sounds "delightfully familiar"; it "reminds me of formal parts of weddings and birthday parties"; or, it is like "thousands of similar events when introducing foreign visitors to university officials. Very typical, delightfully typical." The intercultural dynamics seem to strike a chord. Yet, understanding them is a tall order indeed.

Our understanding has come partly through the ideas of propriety and preparation, in a Finnish version of the play. Finnish propriety means that one should conduct a formal introduction in the proper way, with the appropriate degree of decorum and respect. If possible, one should give the event forethought, learning what one can about the others, and preparing questions that are proper and fitting for the occasion. In fact, the questions used in this encounter—"when did you arrive?," often followed by "When will you leave?," "Have you been meeting people?," "What are you going to do while you are here?"—are very typically used in such exchanges by Finns with foreigners. Moreover, silence and patience in such exchanges is an acknowledged way of giving the occasion its proper due. Exchanges such as these should not be too short, and thus one expects a proper silence, even quietude, as a sign that the occasion is being conducted properly, politely, and respectfully. As many Finns have pointed out, good human relations, like Finnish coffee, take time to brew. Giving the event the proper time makes it that much better, and one cannot hurry the process! So Finnish standards of propriety and preparation are active in a silence, signifying that the visitor and the occasion are being treated respectfully and properly. This is good.

As a result of these cultural premises and preferences, a Finnish interactional sequence can be produced during an introduction: pacing tends to be slower "than Americans tend to do"; verbalizations might be prepared ahead of time; and silence is quite comfortable and acceptable in order to prolong the situation and thus to make it more meaningful and more respectful of social relations. Additionally, there are important nonverbal messages that are difficult to notice from the quoted transcript but are nonetheless worthy of comment. Notice that Mr. Virtanen rises from his desk and walks in front of it to stand directly in front of DC. This is a gesture of respect for the occasion, and the visitor, from Mr. Virtanen. Further, Professors Silvo and Levo are situated at the side of DC. This is a gesture of support by them, of him. More nonverbal subtleties are also active here, including differing uses of the eyes and faces. Noticing these nonverbal actions helps us understand how this event, and scene, was structured in a Finnish way to convey respect and support of DC and the occasion.

A popular American version of this play is different, for there are, of course, other features, other premises and preferences operating. Ideas perhaps active in American professional and business scripts as this may come to the fore, particularly with regard to being introduced, with these guided by an emphasis on quantity, and efficiency. On arriving, one may walk through a hallway and meet a large number of people, the feeling being that one has been greeted by, and introduced to, the whole group. Unlike the Finnish ideas of propriety and respect, an American idea may be "to get to know"—in this way—as many people as quickly as possible. The American interactional script accompanying these ideas may be conducted at a quicker pace, pauses being short; spontaneous verbalizations playing into the scene rather than prescripted comments; and the words, more than the nonverbal actions, being the crucial site of communicative messages. (In a recent visit to an American university, I enacted this kind of script, being introduced to 17 people in 45 minutes.) Against this backdrop, within this American version of the play, silences of even a short duration, "compared to those Finns produce," can be sources of discomfort for some Americans. As one Finnish observer said about the aforementioned exchange, DC "suffers from the pauses!"

We have offered a series of observations on some initial interactions and an intercultural encounter, as these have occurred in actual situations by Americans and Finns. We have interpreted some of the features involved in this one encounter from Finnish and American perspectives. Based on several other similar events, we believe that these features suggest ways of structuring acts and sequences of this kind. We have thus noticed how these communication practices are shaped by cultural premises and preferences, cultural notions of sequencing and further how these practices are explained by participants through cultural terms for those practices such as "getting acquainted with the workplace" and asia-talk in Finnish, or by small talk in American English. Each draws attention to different cultural forms of communication, through sequential enactments and cultural terms, with each identifying kinds of communicative practices being produced. Further, we discussed various cultural premises about verbal and nonverbal action, about what is proper and preferred as communication in such scenes in Finland and the United States. By focusing our attention on specific and actual intercultural interactions like these, by interpreting them through these cultural features, and by exploring some of the premises active in these interactions and terms, we have provided an admittedly partial and suggestive account of Finnish and American communication, by way of introductions.

ENDNOTES

1. The authors acknowledge the helpful suggestions for improving the essay from several students of Finnish culture and communication including Michael Berry, Jaakko Lehtonen, Marjatta Nurmikari Berry, and Liisa Salo-Lee. To them we extend our sincere thanks. An earlier version of the essay appears as: "By Way of Introduction: An American and Finnish Dialogue" (see Carbaugh & Poutiainen, 2000).
2. The names of people and places that we use in this paper have been changed so to honor the confidence of our colleagues.
3. The following transcript is based on a videotape of this intercultural encounter. In the videotape, all participants from the original event are re-enacting the event as they recalled it, based on DC's field notes. Analysis of this transcript is based on this and similar introductions in which DC was involved. For the timed silences on lines 8, 14, 20, and 25, the first number is SP's estimate of a customary length of such a pause, with the second number being the actual time of the pause on the video clip. A Finnish production team produced the video.
4. Uses and interpretations of silence vary not only by speaker, but also by regions within Finland. As a Finnish reader of the essay commented, "a Karelian Finn [from the east] may have filled some of those silences," unlike Virtanen, a Hamé Finn.
5. This is especially difficult when native Finnish speakers are expected not only to speak a second language, but to do things, like a USAmerican English version of "small talk," which is done in that sec-

ond language by its native speakers, but not done quite that way in Finnish. On a related point, Finns themselves can be quite reticent in using their own language. This is a source of the oft-repeated joke, from Finns to others: "Finnish people can be silent in several languages!"

6. It is not unusual for Finnish students to have studied and be fluent in English, Swedish, and German, in addition to Finnish.

7. There is a special Finnish attitude associated with this style; it suggests that the discussion, as such, should be done "without a hurry," in Finnish, *istua rauhassa*. For these observations, we are drawing partly on Richard Wilkins' dissertation work at the University of Massachusetts on "asia-talk" (1999).

8. In Finland and many European countries, Americans are often regarded as superficial because of such behaviors.

﹂4﹄

"Superficial Americans" and "Silent Finns": Finnish and USAmerican Cultures in Social Interaction[1]

After spending several months in Finland, and after a nice afternoon coffee, I was asked the following question by a Finnish friend and colleague: "Would you write something about why Americans are so superficial? We hear this so much from Finns who travel to the United States, and from Germans too." At first, I didn't quite know how to respond to this question. Rather exasperated, I replied, "Well, I could try." I began searching my field notes and focusing my subsequent observations for materials that would allow me both to understand, and then to respond to this question. What follows is the result.

CULTURAL PREMISES IN GREETINGS AND "SMALL TALK"

Kirsti, an 18-year-old Finnish female, had just arrived in the United States as an exchange student. Having been in the United States for two weeks, she had met a few people, including Mary. On a sunny afternoon, as Kirsti walked down Main Street in her adopted American town, she saw Mary.

1. Mary: Hi Kirsti!!! How are you?
2. Kirsti: Thank you, good.
3. Mary: Are you enjoying your stay?
4. Kirsti: Yes, very much.
5. Mary: It's a beautiful (!) day outside isn't it?
6. Kirsti: Yes.
7. They talk for a while longer, then say "Good-bye."

The next day, Kirsti saw Mary across the street. She moved toward Mary smiling and waving at her. Mary smiled and waved in return, but kept walking quickly toward her car. These two exchanges between Kirsti and Mary led Kirsti to conclude, "Americans are friendly, but superficial."

A 22-year-old Finnish female, Ulla, had just returned to Finland from the United States, and had this to say about Americans: "Well, Americans are friendly. There's this small talk thing that they do. It's really nice. The person comes up to you and says 'How are you?' and you talk for a while and it's nice." Immediately she added, "But then they're superficial. I saw this person [whom she had had small talk with the day before] the next day and she just waved and acted like she didn't even know me. I don't understand that."

An American male who was a student at a Finnish University, after hearing this kind of story repeatedly, exclaimed in exasperation, with a hint of anger: "If I hear that Americans are superficial one more time …" Clearly he had heard enough of this kind of thing. The claim by Finns that Americans are superficial is difficult for Americans to hear, as it is also difficult for Finns to hear analogous claims made by Americans about Finns (e.g., "They're so silent and shy").

But what are some of the conversational sources of these claims, these rather negative "national attributions"? How is it that some Finns, on interacting with Americans, find them to be superficial? Perhaps this has something to do with the ways Americans and Finns use their own language, and moreover, it might have something to do with the ways each uses the same language (e.g., English), yet in culturally distinctive ways. Let's explore this possibility in some detail (see Agar, 1994).

In the exchange between Kirsti and Mary, we notice in the first seven lines that the exchange went relatively smoothly. We could also notice in line 2 that Kirsti's comment, "Thank you, good," shows that she might be rather new to uses of English. Where many users of English might say "Fine, thanks" or simply "Good," Kirsti is supplying an utterance close to a Finnish one that is often produced in this conversational place, *Kiitos, hyvin*. But her utterance of "Thank you, good" presents no problem in the exchange. Even if Kirsti is relatively new to English, she appears to be using English quite ably, and nicely converses with Mary in it.

However, the interaction on the following day between Mary and Kirsti might be a source of some puzzlement for Kirsti. On seeing Mary, she presumes Mary will be available for at least some limited conversation. When, however, a simple and hurried wave was supplied by Mary, instead of some verbal exchange, Kirsti was surprised and disappointed. So, if there is some difficulty created in these interactions between Mary and Kirsti, one source of that difficulty might be the differences in the kind of relational groundwork each presumed was getting done in the course of their earlier conversational encounter.[2] What presumably is getting done in this kind of conversation? What is its cultural status, or significance, as an action?

If we take this exchange between Mary and Kirsti, and consider also the comments of Ulla, we might be able to identify one kind of slippage, or asynchrony, between Finnish and American premises for this kind of conversation. It appears a Finnish premise is this: Once one engages in this kind of conversation with another, a "communicative relationship" has been established, such that one is expected to talk—even if briefly—with the other on meeting her again. In other words, if one has already talked with another for a period of time, as in greetings, or in small talk, on meeting them again, there is a slight social obligation to talk with them again (cf. Wieder & Pratt, 1990, 1993). That obligation, if rather weak, presumes both that the initial meeting carried some consequences for action, such that on meeting again, if it is at all possible, one should stop and exchange a few words. That subsequent verbal interaction, when forthcoming, reaffirms a Finnish relational connection as it resolidifies the link with the other that was presumably forged during the earlier, initial exchange. Further, the subsequent interaction reaffirms that the earlier exchange was something important and worthy of one's time and attention. In a sense, then, the earlier, initial conversation can carry more relational significance and interactional consequence in Finnish than in some USAmerican social interaction.

Note the consequences for Kirsti, from this Finnish point of view, when subsequent interaction was not forthcoming, as it was not from Mary, nor apparently not also from other Americans that Ulla encountered. There was some sense of violation (of Finnish expectations) on several counts. As noted, subsequent verbal interaction was not forthcoming (a wave was not sufficient as a subsequent interaction); lacking that, the presumed relational link with the American was called into question (e.g., perhaps we are not becoming friends like I thought we were); further, and in retrospect, the status of the previous small talk was called into question (e.g., it was not what it seemed to be at that earlier time). Considering this kind of Finnish reflection, Americans like Mary and others seem not to enact their interactional obligations at all seriously. As a result, links with Americans can seem to be not just weak but illusory, and exchanges with them to be shallow. Thus, Americans can seem (to Finns) to be, using their term, *superficial.*

There are other possible sources of the Finnish claim about superficial Americans that are evident in the kind of exchange just described. Some of these relate to Finnish cultural rules for speaking. For Finns, especially when in public with people one does not know really well, and even sometimes with close friends, it is important to speak properly. One kind of proper speech, active in the aforementioned conversations and others presented in the previous chapter, is guided by some configuration of these rules:[3]

1. One should not state what is obvious;
2. If speaking, one should say something worthy of everyone's attention;
3. One should not invoke topics or themes that are contentious or conflictual (or more positively, one should keep present relations on harmonious ground);
4. One should be personally committed to or invested in what one says;
5. What you say properly—the unobvious, socially worthwhile, noncontentious, personally involving statements—forms a basis for subsequent interactions and social relations.

These rules can function in a very demanding way. With just the first rule, one feels one ought to say something that is not obvious. This requires some thought, sometimes considerable thought, perhaps in forms of quietude (in Finnish, *mietiskelle* or *omissa oloissaan*), prior to speaking. Add to that, that one ought to say something worthy of the social occasion, and that it ought to be noncontentious, and something that reflects one's personal commitments, one finds one's speech is subject to considerable demands. These conditions, when met, of course constrain the production of talk, making it something that is quite considered and thoughtful, and thus can lay the cultural grounds for a rather potent form of conversation.

When these Finnish conversational rules contact other systems of communication practice, like an American one, difficulties can arise. For example, in the quoted exchange, on a beautiful sunny day, Mary, the American, says, "It's a beautiful day." Finns might think, on the basis of the first Finnish rule, that saying such an obvious thing is "rather silly," and perhaps such things should "go without saying" or "are better left unsaid." After all, as the Finn said to me when we discussed an American propensity to use first names when addressing each other, "Why say such things when they are so damn obvious? I know my name and you know my name so why even mention it?" In social exchanges like these, if engaged in a kind of American small talk, one might hear (and produce) all kinds of comments about obvious things, like "Nice day, huh?," "Got your hair cut," "Rainy isn't it," "Hi, Chuck," that to Finns could, even should "go without saying." Because Americans sometimes talk about such things that are on the surface, and because Finns as a rule generally prefer that public talk go beyond that surface, Americans can seem, to Finns, to be stating the obvious, and thus to be superficial.[4]

Another source of possible intercultural difficulty in the segment can be related to the use of superlatives such as the "beautiful" that Mary spoke on line 5. The free use of superlatives by Americans can sound troubling to some Finnish ears. One Finnish woman who lived in America for a couple of years described an encounter with her American aunt: "She would describe things saying, 'It's magnificent' or 'It's absolutely gorgeous!' When she asked me about something, I would reply genuinely by saying, 'It's nice,' but then my aunt would say, 'Don't you like it?' It would drive me crazy." She went on saying, "I just can't say things like, 'It's so fabulous.' That runs against my grain." If this is a typical pattern, it suggests, relative to Americans, that Finnish uses of such superlatives are less emphatic, or more reserved, if existent at all. This becomes especially the case because uses of superlatives can sound to Finns a bit presumptuous, and can possibly be heard as immodest, or as being too impressionable, reflecting a person whose inner being falls prey to overstatement, or quick, exaggerated, emotional whims. As Mary exclaimed the obvious, "Beautiful day outside," she may have run a bit against Kirsti's Finnish "grain." American uses of superlatives are perhaps, relative to Finns, more frequent and intense, thus giving the impression of saying more, and speaking more intensely, than is necessary, natural, or even accurate. Because Americans can use superlatives very freely, and because Finns may use them less freely and perhaps more cautiously, Americans can sound superficial to Finns, saying more than the social situation perhaps properly and rightfully warrants.

With the aforementioned patterns in mind, we have now established perhaps a better understanding of the sources of the Finnish claim that Americans are, at times, superficial. Part of the sense of this judgment is built on Finnish standards of practice that are used to evaluate communication by Finns, and Americans. The standards evident so far are: (a) That people who engage in talk incur a slight obligation to continue a communicative relationship; (b) that people should not freely and continually state the obvious; and (c) that people should not overstate the case. Americans, on some occasions, as we have seen in this and chapter 3, can violate all of these Finnish expectations, or rules. This gives some cultural grounds to the attribution of superficiality from the vantage point of Finnish patterns of communication.

FRIENDLINESS: A COMMUNAL FORM OF MEMBERSHIP

Presumably Americans, who act as previously mentioned, are not trying to be superficial, nor would they say they claim a value in superficiality.

What, then, are these Americans doing, in their terms? Or, what are their expressed intentions—implicitly and explicitly—when conversing this way? What features of American communication are evident here?

In contemporary America, encounters like the one between Mary and Kirsti are quite common. People greet, and follow up their greetings with a friendly wave, or perhaps other exchanges about things that are often quite obvious like the weather, current events, and visible personal effects (e.g., a book one is reading, clothes). The functions of such encounters are varied, but perhaps generally, in America, they have something to do simply with verbally acknowledging the existence of each participant (thus the frequent use of first names), and establishing a momentary link between them (thus the importance given to "relationships"). The tone is typically quite friendly. And often in the process, given the backdrop of variety in types of people in the American scene today (e.g., Blacks, Anglos, Hispanics, Native Americans, Chinese, Vietnamese, Irish, German, Italian, East Indian, etc.), the result is the verbal demonstration or disclosure of some common experience. Because people in America are presumably different and unique, both culturally and personally, such encounters are not trivial, but substantial efforts to acknowledge the presence of each other, and to forge some kind of civil links among them. Friendly interaction, therefore, as this, is forceful culturally partly because it so often occurs against a culturescape of considerable variety and difference. American "friendliness" thus should not be confused with "friendship," for the former is required routinely in public encounters with an eye to linking people who are presumably different, whereas the latter stems from other forms of action, deemed more personal than public. Philipsen (1989) called this kind of linking, a display of shared membership in a group, the communal function of communication. We can hear this, here, as people comport themselves through a kind of "friendly banter of small talk."

After engaging in such civil, sociable encounters, the obligation one incurs to follow them up is, relative to Finns, quite minimal, if existent. One might engage in similar encounters with the same people again, but one would typically feel a minimal obligation to do so. If possible, or timely, one might converse with others one has met earlier only briefly, but such would be done more out of kindness or courtesy, and less because one would feel a relational duty to meet with them. If other encounters are to move from "civil" to "personal," or if they are, as some Americans put it, to "go anywhere," that is, if they are to incur some felt obligation of participants to each other, they do so through other forms of communication.

Some recent research into American communication patterns has demonstrated that Americans differentiate "small talk" from "really communicating" (Cameron, 2000; Carbaugh 1988b; Katriel & Philipsen, 1981; Philipsen 1992). Small talk or chitchat, as perhaps was that between Mary and Kirsti, is generally less valued than "real communication," and is, relative to it, rather closed, distant, neutral, and rigid. To many Americans, chitchat is important as a form of sociability, but it is also less valued, less potent relationally, and less penetrating as a means of self-expression. As a result, engaging in it incurs little by way of obligation.

Some rules that Americans use and invoke when speaking in public are quite different from those supplied by Finns for similar public contexts. Americans believe that one should express one's self, with very few constraints being placed on that expressiveness. In fact, participants often state the rule that people are free to say whatever they please, and it is not up to those present—thinking perhaps it is only "up to God"—to evaluate or judge those expressions (see Carbaugh, 1988b; and Hymes, 1986). Such rules lay bases for great amounts of talk, because the belief is that everyone should have the opportunity to speak, or be heard from. Such speaking often elaborates one's personal experiences, thoughts, and feelings. Americans are often, in public speech, then, less preoccupied with the social worthiness of their expression, than they are with its personal importance. An American system can play on the sensed need, on one hand, to produce talk as a basis for common civil life, and on the other, to treat the unique circumstances of individuals as the basic theme in such talk. Together, the dynamic produces much public talk that is close to the surface and incurs little by way of future interactional obligations, but does so as an important means of producing public information, common resources, and a social mosaic of differences, if in a less than deeply penetrating way (Carbaugh, 2002).

The American rules for speaking can create much talk that is, from the vantage point of the Finnish system, quite suspect. Saying things that are obvious, paying more attention to personal matters, and less attention to the social worthiness of a topic of discussion they introduce, all of this can appear superficial to Finns. This might be because Americans often talk as if they presume very little in common among those present. Furthermore, some Americans might playfully speak contentiously, introducing a controversial topic in order "to get someone or something going," to turn up the heat and intensity of an ongoing social encounter. Offense at this is not necessarily taken, in fact some even delight at the airing of diverse and competing views. And more puzzling perhaps, to many Finns, is the extent to which some Americans might say things (e.g., make proposals or propositions) that they do not agree with at all, or are not all that personally committed to, or invested in. Such talk is sometimes used to test ideas, or as a mode of thought (e.g., "thinking out loud"), than it is a demonstration of one's deeper convictions or beliefs. These American rules, when in use, can produce many and varied personal disclosures and opinions, assertions that are not personally held, obvious statements and the like, for the sake of generating information and discussion. Yet all of this, from the outside, can also be easily heard as lacking depth and conviction, thus being superficial.

So, are Americans superficial when they fail to follow up social encounters, speak about the obvious, make statements they don't necessarily believe in, and overstate for the sake of discussion, or argument? From a Finnish point of view perhaps. But if taken as intended, from their own "American" frame of reference, they are up to something else: Getting the conversation going; providing some necessary information; airing a diversity of views; in the process, acknowledging each other's presence and linking with each other; exhibiting some common life, some form of civility, if sometimes preoccupied with personal themes, or if sometimes contentious. Such is often done in the spirit of friendliness, of getting along with each other, even if this doesn't appear, from the outside, to go very deep.

The depth of such American encounters is not necessarily in the content of these conversations—they can produce many varied reactions—but in their cultural forms. Through these forms of social life, a common forum for American people is created, a forum where anyone can have a say, where a civil routine is created, where information is produced, and differences among people are both a warrant and theme in its production. This might appear peculiar from abroad, as it sometimes does from within, but the pieces of it that might seem that way from afar are a part of another puzzle closer to its home. There, the larger picture is one that presumes verbal information should be freely available, and great differences among people must be heard. Thus talk about things that are never deemed all that obvious becomes part of a form that routinely creates a common life. This picture, a mosaic in motion, of course differs from others, painted in other places. In Finland, the picture is perhaps one that presumes people hold much in common, and thus should not be preoccupied with the obvious surfaces of life, the all-too-apparent commonness of things, but should move beyond that.

These are preliminary observations that need much further consideration. Yet hopefully they demonstrate ways that communication is patterned in culturally distinctive ways. For example, they show how similar forms of sociable speaking, especially initial encounters, are erected on culturally distinctive premises; they show that rules for producing sociable speech vary from cultural communicative system to cultural communicative system; they show that the use and interpretation of particular linguistic devices like superlatives vary in culturally distinctive ways; and finally, they show that each of these differences can be a source of miscommunication and negative cultural stereotypes.

With regard to the relationship between language use and culture, note that the example given demonstrates how a single language, in this case, English, is presuming two different cultural meaning systems. In the other direction, the Finnish language could also be used to express American and, of course, Finnish cultures. The crucial variable when treating culture and communication is not only the language being used, although this is itself profoundly important, but the patterned ways in which a language is being used, and the cultural meanings associated with it. This requires careful description of social interaction, and nonverbal means of expression, as shown in the conversational scenes expressed. It requires further that one interpret the cultural meanings that are being presumed by and created in those interactions, with those means of expression. Although the cultural interpretation in the aforementioned is somewhat preliminary, a deeper look would explore what such patterns implicate by way of beliefs about being a person, about societal life, and acting with others. In the process, we can come to hear cultures in linguistic, and nonlinguistic, action, to hear what such interaction presumes, what it says and means. Such leads can help develop our understanding of our own cultural conduct, and that of others, while also enabling a better understanding of the dynamics that transpire when one cultural system of expression contacts another. With these objectives in mind, let's look a bit deeper into these features of Finnish and American interactions.

MASS-MEDIATING CULTURES:
A FINNISH AND USAMERICAN CONVERSATION
(with Michael Berry, *Turku School of Economics and Business, Finland*)

Here we turn briefly to a televised interview, between Finns and an American, a further example of intercultural interaction, which will allow us to deepen our understanding of Finnish and USAmerican communication. We present this particular segment for several reasons: It involves an instance of intercultural communication that is public, even popular. In it, there are cultural forms at play for identifying self and other. Each such form is demonstrably part of different cultural discourses, with each being "fashioned" in its own cultural way, while also being "read" in another way from the point of view on another cultural discourse. Like the third-party introduction in chapter 3 and the greeting segment between Mary and Kirsti, this interview is thus about, and is also conducted through, different cultural features and forms.

The following segment was part of a televised episode titled, *"Tango Finlandia,"* which was shown initially in February of 1993 on the American program, *60 Minutes.* Since then, the episode has been rebroadcast every year in the United States, making it the most frequently shown episode in the history of what is arguably the most successful USAmerican television program ever made. We have been trying to understand, among other things, why this episode has so captivated its viewers on both sides of the Atlantic by exploring the ways it both exhibits, and inhabits, popular American and popular Finnish discourses. It is also significant, for our purposes, that this same episode has been broadcast in Finland, in Finnish, in the fall of 1999. With that brief background, consider the following segment, hosted by *60 Minutes* correspondent, Morley Safer, which begins with Safer interviewing the first Finnish speaker in the episode, Jan Knutas.[5]

40. Jan Knutas:
41.   We're a silent (.) brooding *hh people.
42.   We think a lot.
43.   We like to ((lip smack)) keep our privacy *h
44.   and give (.5)
45.   the fellow man (.5)
46.   his privacy
47.   keep a distance.
48. Morley Safer: (Voiceover)
49.   Jan Knutas is a Finnish author and producer for the
50.   government radio service *hh
51.   Finns, he says (.)
52.   have a difficult time making even
53.   the most **casual**? social contact *h
54.   with a stranger on a bus for example.
55. Knutas (Cut to interview with Safer)
56.   I begin to think that *hhh
57.   I hope (.5)
58.   the other person doesn't say something ~I
59.   might have to engage in a
60.   conversation now *hhhh hh
61.   it's (.) it's a horrifying thought
62.   and sometimes you have to~
63. (Footage of Jan Knutas and Morley Safer)
64.   He actually says that *hhh

65.   where are you going *h

66.   And then it's oh god I have to talk now *hhh

67.   even if I would like to say (.)

68.   please leave me alone

69.   and let me brood for an hour *hhhhh uhhh

70.   aaaa I'm too polite to do that, so I go along (1)

71.   and get irritated in the process.

What we wish to highlight here are the ways in which this particular segment includes forms of social interaction that are culturally distinctive, and that create, through cultural discourses—a system of cultural premises, preferences, and rules—a sense of the "other" as a stranger, or of "otherness" as strange.

Note first how this segment appeared as an early part of an American "news" program, *60 Minutes;* thus, it employed a kind of journalistic interview between an American (Safer) and a Finn (Knutas). Both participants are public figures, Knutas, a Finnish media figure and Safer, an American journalist, respectively. We draw attention, then, to begin, to a form of social interaction at work here, the interview, and to those participants explicitly being identified in it, Safer, the American journalist (identified earlier in the broadcast), and Knutas, the Finnish media personality (so identified on lines 49 and 50).

Second, this form of social interaction is being conducted in culturally distinctive ways. For example, the response of Knutas (lines 41 through 47 and lines 57 through 71) is highly cultural in what is said (e.g., we are silent, brooding, distant Finns), in how this is being structured (e.g., demands to talk are irritating), in the stance from which it is structured (e.g., an expansion on the thoughts of silence, and the fears about verbal interaction with strangers), and in what is presumed by this way of addressing a foreign other (e.g., we know Americans don't brood, but do like to talk, often speak without thinking, and may not think much even when silent). In short, Knutas' response is a Finnish way of telling non-Finns, especially Americans, about being a Finn. His utterance constructs Finnish features in a way that implicitly contrasts those features with common Finnish conceptions of Americans. This kind of report Knutas provides, about a Finnish cultural self to (an American) other, is a well-known practice to some Finns, and is done (by Knutas) perhaps unaware that the other (Safer) might misunderstand what is being said from this Finnish view. Also, Knutas is acting Finnish in nonverbal ways including his "lip smack" on line 43, and in his use of his eyes.

Safer, on the other hand, conducts the interview through a rather bemused posture and face. In this way he draws attention to—what he considers—perplexing and peculiar features of this cultural other (lines 51 through 54). In the process, he assumes a journalistic stance that is bemused at cultural difference (demonstrated by Safer's facial expressions). Perhaps further, although Safer acts bemused, perhaps he is unaware of the degree to which this emotion is indeed working, here—Safer perhaps does not know that Knutas is giving a culturally stylized report, even a playful report about Finnish character, thus he (i.e. Safer) misses both that the report is specially designed to pique an American ear (or eye), and is built through a caricature of Finnish traits and character (well known, of course, to Finns).

These second observations, therefore, suggest that the interview form here includes Finnish and American versions, with each adopting a different cultural stance, and with each casting the other, and the self, in different lights. As a result, the interview demonstrates how features of this conversation create an intercultural communicative event that is being conducted (in part) according to locally distinctive rules, forms, preferences, and premises for interviewing, in this case, on TV (see also Briggs, 1986; Carbaugh, 1990c, 1993c).

Third, the interview segment has been edited in cultural ways. This involves playing with basic elements in these forms of social interaction, such that the initial real-time sequences are being reversed, with specific visual images being strategically supplied—albeit from an American view. For example, regarding the resequencing of this talk, Safer can be heard, on lines 52 through 54, to be paraphrasing Knutas, yet this occurs prior to Knutas' comment that is, most likely, being paraphrased (lines 56 through 71). In this way, Safer's earlier comment provides, in the video text, a verbal frame for Knutas' comment, making it (Knutas' comment) sound like a Finnish confirmation of Safer's interpretation, rather than its earlier motivation. The visual images surrounding this segment, literally, complete this picture by showing Finnish people on a bus looking (shying?) away from the camera, suggesting this as an appropriate image for "the horrifying thought" Knutas mentions, and the "difficult time making ... social contact" alluded to by Safer. Knutas' and Safers' words, along with these images, create a message, at least for some American viewers, that Finns like to "brood" alone, and don't want to engage in casual social–visual–verbal contact.

Within a Finnish discourse, however, Knutas' comments do something else. They describe not a people's character, but social practices in which the form of social interaction referred to here as "brooding" might be used. This kind of Finnish understanding rests on several cultural premises: For example, that Knutas' report is a way of reporting about Finns to Finns, and to non-Finns; that this kind of report activates in its utterance a Finnish respect for privacy; and that privacy and a certain distance among people can mean not only respect for others but moreover a positive valuing of quietude or silence. These Finnish premises are, for Finns, knowingly expressed in Knutas' comment here. However, these premises are not salient or relevant in U.S. viewers' discourse about the segment, nor evidently in their hearing of Knutas' words. In this sense, the segment again demonstrates different cultural preferences for forms of social interaction, different premises about ways of reporting cultural self to others, and different rules for conducting social interaction in public. In other words, the very same words, forms, and visual images play into, or inhabit different cultural discourses, thus invoking different codes and meanings.

Finally, this segment appears within a larger "American" journalistic story. One typical version of this story involves the cultural casting or representation of another as puzzling, in this case, "the silent, expressionless Finn." Of course, the puzzling other is so, only as a negation of one's self, the "talkative outgoing American." This is followed by a presumed remedy—from a popular American view—that this other needs a socially expressive outlet. The American video segment presents the Tango as a curiosity, for it is apparently such an outlet for the Finns. Yet, even with this outlet, or even while dancing the Tango, Finns are depicted as depressed (through the theme of the Tango lyrics) and, relative to Americans, inexpressive emotionally. As these parts of the story are shown, the segment feeds a grand American journalistic narrative about the curious and perplexing ways of another, reaffirming a U.S. stance that the "other" is perplexing, while offering little by way of understanding that other, from the Finnish point of view.

USAMERICAN AND FINNISH DISCURSIVE CODES

Our observations show how this segment, and story, is being read into, as well as being produced within broader Finnish, and U.S. discourses. Our more detailed analyses demonstrate how American viewers' reactions to the episode follow this discursive sequence: We're baffled; Finns are inexplicably inexpressive, sad, and shy; this has to be a problem for them (we can perhaps attribute the problem to the gloomy northern weather, cold temperature, and lack of sun); here's our solution (rather than Tango, Finns need to share their feelings, and communicate). American cultural premises underlie this discursive sequence, and presume a particular model for the person: Be an expressive individual who communicates openly and expresses feelings warmly and freely.

The very same words and images are read into a different, Finnish cultural discourse. Reactions to the episode are formed through the

Finnish discourse in this way: We don't know whether to laugh or cry, some of us are very angry, some of us are humored, some of us are humored and angry. If there's humor, it's because Knutas is doing Finnish satire here, a black self-deprecating humor. As a result, he's funny, but not to all Finns, because his jokes are based on an exaggeration of cultural truths, values, and understandings that we Finns share among ourselves. However, others, especially Americans, don't understand these things about Finns. Popular Finnish premises underlie this discourse, for it presumes a particular model for the person: Speak when one has something to say that is worthy of others' consideration. Otherwise, be a silent, respectful, and reserved person who can and should watch and listen, with emotions best being expressed subtly, and nonverbally (see Auer-Rizzi & Berry, 2000; Berry, 1997; Carbaugh, 1994a; Lehtonen & Sajavaara, 1985; Nurmikari-Berry & Berry, 1999; Sajavaara & Lehtonen, 1997).

To summarize, this televised segment is part of what we might call a generic interactional form, *the interview*. In it, we can notice different cultural stances for interviewing and being interviewed. As a result, the same forms, words, and images, are crafted from and carry into different cultural discourses, with different meanings. Chief among these meanings are premises for how to present one's culture to others, as well as what is culturally valued in that presentation for being a person. Through our interviews with Knutas, we must add that Knutas clearly knows, and caters to, both American and Finnish cultural discourses, and plays some Finnish themes in a Finnish way. He knows further that (U.S.) foreigners (especially) may not only puzzle over this, but also delight in it. We must also add that Knutas did not expect his "play" to be readily misunderstood, or unappreciated by some Finns, which it was. A difficult consequence of this play is that, first, American viewers rarely, if ever, get his joke. Finnish viewers may or may not get the joke and if it is noticed, it may not be appreciated at all. As in all such play, there are serious, even dangerous, elements at work (see Basso, 1979).

Part of the seriousness in this type of intercultural conversation is the introduction and cultivation, within an American discourse, of a perplexity about Finnishness. Viewers are left with an impression that Finns, or others, are not like Americans, and are offered little by way of understanding who "they" are, from the Finnish view. With a little more knowledge, and perhaps a little less drama, the broadcast could have elaborated on some of the positive Finnish values in quietude, privacy, and respect, but did not. Furthermore, had the part of Knutas' interview that preceded line 41 not been deleted from the broadcast, his reference to silence, privacy, and solitude would have sent a different message, for in this prior segment, he discussed Finns as honest and conscientious people who never play roles and are trustworthy. In other words, rather than speaking sociably to surface matters, he was describing Finns as *hiljaisia, mietiskeleviää* [quiet, thinking people]. This, of course, provides a different context for interpreting and producing his subsequent comments beginning on line 41.

The intercultural dynamics at play at this point are complicated further by differences between languages, between popular American English and Finnish. For example, the American English term, *brooding* (line 41) is quite unlike related Finnish terms such as *mietiskellää*, which positively connotes a deeper, studied thoughtfulness, in silence.

There are deep intricacies in these segments of introductions, greetings, and interviewing, between the cultural moves getting done here and the linguistic resources at work. Exploring diverse cultures in conversation through these codes helps remind us that social typifications like "superficial" and "silent," and cultural typifications like "Americans" and "Finns," derive from, and are given shape and meaning within, conversational sequences (like introductions, greetings, and interviews) and the specific acts within those sequences (like reporting about self to others and public nonverbal conduct). Keeping the cultural bases—the rules, preferences, and premises—of these forms, events, and acts in view, can help move our theorizing from abstract considerations of individuals and structures to actual cultural and communicative practices. By treating social interactions as cultural accomplishments, we can draw attention further to the communal features that are active within them (see Braithwaite, 1997; Carbaugh, 1996b; Fitch, 1998; Hastings, 2000; Katriel, 1991; Milburn, 2000; Philipsen, 1989, 1992). We can show better how different codes provide different accounts or explanations for producing and interpreting conversation—and communication—generally. We can also understand better how televised texts such as this one, which are distributed globally, are deeply and distinctively active in local cultural discourses. In the process, we can come to know not just typified persons, but cultural features in conversation. While the world may appear smaller as transmissions of communication span the globe, people nonetheless live, think, and act at least partly through their local cultures in conversation.

ENDNOTES

1. Some of the analyses in this and the following chapter have benefitted from Richard Wilkins' (1999) research on the Finnish style of *asia* [matter-of-fact] talk. An earlier version of the first part of this essay was published originally as: "Are Americans Really Superficial?: Notes on Finnish and American Cultures in Linguistic Action" (see Carbaugh, 1994a).

2. The observations made here of Finnish conversational features are very preliminary and tentative, and are based on field work currently in progress.

3. These rules were inductively derived from field materials and published initially in 1993. Subsequent presentations of them by me and several Finnish speakers to Finnish audiences suggests they have some rather strong utility for capturing Finnish claims of what is good public communication.

4. The formulation of these rules is the subject of additional future research. The rules do however seem linked to what some Finns call "the no-name culture" or the minimal use of personal names, to a general devaluing of small talk (as Americans produce it), to a unique Finnish form of small talk, to many uses of pauses (because of the need to produce proper speech), to Finnish themes of modesty, and distance, as well as to the cultural status of talk itself.

5. The following transcript uses these conventions: lines are broken to indicate cadence and intonation; (.) indicates an audible pause with those longer recorded in seconds; hhh is an audible breath; **boldface** indicates emphasis; a period indicates falling intonation; the ~ indicates a linking of sound with the following utterance.

⫷ 5 ⫸

"Self," "Soul," and "Sex": Russian and USAmerican Cultures in a Televised Conversation

TALK SHOWS, SELVES, AND CULTURES

The idea of a "talk show," if not exclusively American, has been cultivated in a distinctively American way for at least three decades. The current plethora of offerings in this televised genre is truly mind-boggling. Part of the intrigue, I think, is that these programs showcase the audience and are thus built, at least in part, on the performance of audience members. In the 1960's, the first popular show in the genre, *Donahue*, seized the day by placing a segment of the audience typically deemed unworthy of air time—homemakers and the unemployed who were home watching at 9:00 a.m.—right in front of the cameras, and thus gave them the opportunity to speak to the issues of the day. Although the topics being addressed over the years have changed, one fact has not: Whatever topic is addressed (from sex to foreign policy to male born-again Christian go-go dancers), it is the audience reaction to the topic, as much as it is the topic itself, or the scheduled guests, that makes the talk show what it is. Without this audience participation, this display of the people's thoughts and feelings, there would be no talk show as it has come to be known in the United States today.

This widespread display of participation in televised talk has captivated a huge public, and cultivated certain beliefs and values. Chief among these are particular beliefs about a kind of public discourse. In other words, the "talk" that is being "shown," that unwieldy discursive formation, has itself assumed a life of its own. Typically, with this public discourse, it has become rather common for people to stand before millions and freely speak their mind (or "share their feelings"), for others to grant them the "right" to do this, and for many to believe that this is something important—or at least entertaining—to do (to "talk it out"). That this discursive production is a rather recent accomplishment, that it is the particular workings of a particular American culture, that it is prominent in televised conduct, and that its enactment displays particular beliefs and values about public discourse (and proper uses of television) warrants our vigilant attention.

In the process of showing this kind of "talk," and through the participation of the common folk in it, the talk show also has cultivated certain cultural beliefs about the person. Some of these beliefs about the person can be summarized in this way: As one believes that speaking up—or speaking out—is important and valued, an attendant belief is cultivated in being one who so speaks. As earlier studies have shown (Carbaugh, 1988b, 2002), implicated in this televised discourse is a message: One should "be honest" and "share feelings" in public, and these acts should foreground the seemingly endless flaws of society (or its oppressive institutions or corrupt corporations). In the process of televising this kind of talk, the talk show has thus also cultivated certain beliefs about the person, or self.

The media of communication can be conceptualized, similarly, as operating fundamentally on the bases of the particular beliefs of particular social and cultural communities. If beliefs about public discourse and persons vary by community and scene, so the argument would go, then so too do beliefs about the media of communication. The media, however, do not just vary in how they are used, but more fundamentally in their very nature, what different people believe the media are, what they can and should be, and how each segment of the media should be used. For example, whether television (or a genre of it, or a particular program) is conceived as a conduit to a "real" world, as an instrument of a corporation, a tool of a nation state, or as a window into the spiritual (and all of these hold considerable weight somewhere), this makes a radical difference. Cultural beliefs about televisual media thus establish a complex frame for what is shown (what it "is" one believes one is seeing or hearing), and for how that "show" should be interpreted (seen and heard). In other words, the media of communication—as selves—are conceived and used based on the social and cultural premises of community life. To take this seriously, then, we must treat any medium of communication not just as a neutral technology *en masse* that is laminated with various cultural features, but moreover as an organic plant whose very roots and fruits may shift depending on the cultural soil in which it is planted. From this angle, as the distinctive cultural foundations of the media (and selves) shift, so too does their very fundamental nature in social and communal life.

Starting here, and granting there are other places to start, and by focusing on a "Spacebridge" that is rooted in Russian and American soils, I explore how different beliefs about persons, public discourse, and the media, get woven into a single televised episode. Demonstrated, I hope, are some of the sociocultural variations that make public communication, and thus televised communication (as well as selves), fundamentally different in different cultural scenes (Carbaugh, 1996b, 2002). Reflecting these commitments, the analyses presented here explore conversations, "media and selves," as the "talk show"—as an intensive performance of a kind of communally based, organic cultural discourse.

ETHNOGRAPHY AND PEOPLES' CULTURAL CONVERSATIONS

Media scholar, Justin Lewis (1991), summarized his review of audience research with this basic finding: "We now know that the power to produce meanings lies neither within the TV message nor within the viewer, but in the active engagement between the two" (p. 58). He elaborates: "Television's power lies in the specificities of its encounter with the audience. One cannot exist without the other" (p. 61). Using an interview-based methodology, Lewis then goes on to discuss various social meanings of various television texts. He highlights the problem of interpreting viewer's meanings of texts, and relations among those various meanings, by typifying these as uniform, oppositional, or resistant.

The ethnographic approach taken in this chapter addresses also the problem of linking viewers and particular TV messages. As Lewis (1991) puts it, it addresses "the specificities of [TV's] encounter with the audience" (p. 61). As with the exploration of the *60 Minutes* segment in the previous chapter, this current study does so by treating particular television texts, not as something *sui generis*, but as part of a larger expressive system that a group or community interprets and uses. By exploring that expressive system, one gains a particular perspective from which to interpret the (sometimes various) ways that community views telemedia and their meanings. The approach suggests a shifting of focal concerns, then, from viewers to cultural communities, and from TV messages to the cultural discourses (of beliefs and values) they bring to, or "see" with or hear on TV. By foregrounding cultural communities and their discourses, their own beliefs about communication, and using those beliefs to interpret televisual media (and selves), one can conduct a kind of audience research that is anchored, conceptually and methodologically, not in one televised "text," but in a community's discourse system (including television). The conceptual shifts—from viewer to community, from text to expressive system—carry with them, certain methodological consequences. How does one design and execute this type of research?

Given the aims of this study, the following procedures were employed. A first phase of analysis was fairly open and exploratory and involved these various tasks: (a) detailed readings about each culture, its customs, beliefs, and ways of living; (b) observing Russian (and others from former Soviet states) speakers, students, various Russian interactions with Americans, Russian's stories about contacts with Americans, American's stories about contacts with Russians; (c) recording on video, creating, and procuring verbal transcripts of several hours of Russian and American exchanges that were televised, as well as not televised; (d) and, a first phase of interviewing that explored some of the aforementioned observations, focusing at times on moments of asynchrony or confusion between the two in order to understand what was common and different about each community's expressive systems. This procedure created some sense of the general discursive terrain that each group traveled.

A second phase of analysis was very focused. For this phase, I selected specific televised texts that exhibited some of the general cultural dynamics just formulated. Each was transcribed, and analyzed first by me alone, extending the preliminary analyses developed in phase one. Next, I arranged for Russian consultants (alone), then American consultants (alone) to watch these segments with me. I recorded our co-viewings on audio tape, then we listened to ourselves watching, so to speak, as another source of data. This proved to be extremely valuable, for our reactions were always keyed directly to specific moments in the televised texts. Finally, I selected one televised text for intensive analyses, the one my co-investigators and I came to understand as the most "rich" or culturally dense from the vantage point of both systems (a transcript of this text is included on pp. 62–65). As a final procedure, I conducted focused interviews based on a detailed transcript of this text, its viewing by Russians and Americans, and the audio recordings of these co-viewings. The focused analyses of this second phase were linked consistently (by myself and the consultants) to the general themes, dynamics, and difficulties formulated.

Following this process produced an interpretation of Russian and American conversational rituals, and meaning systems, as these interpenetrate this particular scene of the "Spacebridge." The resulting analyses, then, focus not so much on television and viewers, as they do on communal conversations and cultural selves, that is, on cultural discourses viewers use both in the text itself, and to render the television texts meaningful, in their own way. Hopefully this way of approaching the matter demonstrates some of the potential for an ethnographic understanding of conversation and selves in a mediated world.

CONVERSATION AND CULTURAL SELVES

The general capacity to be bound by moral rules may well belong to the individual, but the particular set of rules which transforms him into a human being derives from requirements established in the ritual organization of social encounters.

—Erving Goffman, 1967, p. 45

Conversation, as understood here, is everywhere a culturally situated accomplishment, shaped as it is by local codes, local expressions of what persons and social relations are (and should be), what persons can (and should) do and what, if anything, can (and should) be felt. But nowhere do participants invoke the same codes, the same currents of culture, on all conversational occasions. Nor anywhere do these necessarily situate all participants in the same way. This latter dynamic—of cross-currents in talk—is especially pronounced on intercultural and multicultural occasions when various communication codes—various beliefs about persons, actions, and feelings—become deeply perplexing one to the other.[1]

The televised "Spacebridge" of focal concern in this chapter includes a stream of discourse in which two different cultural currents are flowing, one Russian (or, prior to 1991, largely Soviet), the other American.[2] The general theoretical approach informing the study of this occasion is elaborated here and elsewhere.[3] The analytical problem is one of hearing cultural systems in conversation, with the general response being one of treating seriously participants' own terms, the dimensions and domains of meaning they invoke, their cultural forms of expression, indigenous conversational rules (or structuring norms), and the premises about persons, actions, and feelings implicated in these. These concepts, together, provide a general lens with which to view (or hear) culturally based expressive systems, with each separately bringing into focus a more specific theoretical concern with regard to particular televised moments. Through the application of the general framework, distinctive cultural currents in this conversation are discovered, with each being a local theory for conducting and interpreting this particular communicative action. The case thus demonstrates the workings of a general theoretical approach, the fruits of which unveil culturally situated discourses, as these apply to a segment of television.

The title of this chapter, and book, invites reflection on the concept of *culture* while suggesting that whatever culture is, indeed for the title to make full sense, it is something which is implicated, employed, or creatively invoked in conversation. Treated this way, conversation is at times a cultural accomplishment and, in turn, culture at such times animates, lives in, or provides tangible resources for conversation. From this view, then, culture is not a physical place, a social group of people, nor a whole way of living, although it does create, when used, mutually intelligible senses of place, persons, and patterns of living. What culture is, from this view, is a system of expressive practices that is fraught with feeling, and grandly implicates beliefs about persons, places, and patterns of living. When culture is creatively invoked in conversation, be it on television, in talk about television, or in other scenes of social life—with convergences among these suggesting rich cultural themes—it alerts interlocutors to their common life, its particularities of place, people, and patterns of life, whether these exist in conflict or harmony.

Ethnographic studies of communication, like the kind being done here, have examined the cultural patterning of communicative activity within specific social situations and communities.[4] Again, as some investigators have pointed out, no ethnographic work has yet been done that involves a cultural interpretation of face-to-face, or televised intercultural interaction.[5] The present study is warranted, then, because it explores (a) a televised, conversational segment, (b) in which different cultural systems come into contact, which yields (c) initial interpretations of Russian public communication (and the Russian "soul"), with further attention to American patterns of communication (and its sense of "self"), and reveals (d) some deep sources of difference in this televised medium.

The particular segment examined in this chapter[6] appeared as part of a week-long series titled, "Donahue in Russia." The series was taped in Moscow and broadcast in the United States during the week of February 9, 1987. The particular segment of concern to us here consists of the first 3 minutes and 40 seconds of the second program in the series.[7] Other than a brief "talk-over" by Phil Donahue (lasting 16.8 sec), the segment—following Donahue's normal production format—underwent no postproduction editing. Because this segment displays a generic form of ritualized face work, it is ideally suited for interactional analysis.[8] Because it involves different cultures being creatively employed to guide, evaluate, and justify actions, it is ideally suited for ethnographic study. Because it was seen by Russians and Americans to be a televised expression both troubling and rich, it is ideally suited for a kind of media study. If the following analyses attain some degree of success, that is, if different cultural features are unveiled, readers should be better positioned to hear and see how cultural selves have shaped this conversation and thus be better positioned to understand why, as one informant (bilingual in Russian and English) put it, "They think they're talking about the same thing, but they're not." What, in this televised conversation, has lead this person to this conclusion?

How could she hear in this encounter (as did others who are members of both communities) not just one, but two very different systems operating? How does one hear in this, and other televised conversations, culture(s) at work?

RITUAL AND CULTURAL DISCOURSES

Some conversational episodes foreground a particular interactional goal: the remedy of improprieties. More than anyone, Goffman has drawn our attention to the ritualized form of this type of corrective process:

> When the participants in an undertaking or encounter fail to prevent the occurrence of an event that is expressively incompatible with the judgments of social worth that are being maintained, and when the event is of the kind that is difficult to overlook, then the participants are likely to give it accredited status as an incident—to ratify it as a threat that deserves direct official attention—and to proceed to try to correct for its effects. At this point one or more participants find themselves in an established state of ritual disequilibrium or disgrace, and an attempt must be made to reestablish a satisfactory ritual state for them.
>
> —Goffman, 1967, p. 19

Typically, claims Goffman, such corrective processes follow a rather loosely bound generic sequence, such that an exigence is created through an impropriety; it is socially identified, then further publicized; the publicity precipitates an offering of corrections by the violator(s); which is subsequently accepted (or not), leading to the reestablishment of what Goffman calls "the expressive order" (or its continuing negotiation, or disruption).[9]

Let us look briefly at the ritual Donahue invokes here, then at the Russian one which engulfs him.[10] It is no surprise that Donahue, in his opening segment, initiates discussion with a version of the ritual form which is familiar to him and his American audience. In his first utterances on lines 1–2, 4, 6–7, 11–12, 24–25, Donahue inquires about sex, contraceptive use, pregnancy, and virginity. Topics such as these, Donahue presumes, provide an exigence for public discourse, just as similar topics do in his homeland, erected on the communal assumption, in Bitzer's (1968) terms, that there is an "imperfection marked by urgency" (p. 10). In this case, presumably, the imperfection consists of unwanted pregnancies and perhaps irresponsible premarital sex.[11] The scene is a rhetorical one in that Donahue presumes it can be positively modified, with a partial remedy possibly

1a) DONAHUE: Would you kindly stand for one second, please?

2a) You had sex, when you were 18 years old?

3a) SOVIET MALE A (trans.): Yes, that's when I started.
   b) (.........................)
   c) (.........................)

4a) D: Did you use contraceptive when you practiced sex at age 18?
   [Audience laughter]

5a) SMA (trans.): Yes.
   b) Yes.
   c) Да.

6a) D: Did you take care of this matter yourself or did the girl insist that
7a)   you do it?

8a) SMA (trans.): Yeah, I knew about it before.
   b) Well (.) I knew it before that (.)
   c) Ну я до этого знал

9a) Before that I knew quite a bit.
   b) I knew a lot before that (.)
   c) Я до того знал уже многое
   [PAN TO AUDIENCE LAUGHTER, SMILES]

10a) I knew how, when, what, etc. I was well prepared.
   b) Well before I knew how, what, why (.) I was well prepared.
   c) Ну до этого знал и как, что, чего... Был хорошо подготовлен.

11a) D: Are most Soviet boys conscientious, like you, in protecting the
12a)   girl from pregnancy?

13a) SMA (trans.): Basically, yes. Why don't you ask the others?
   b) Yes (.) basically, yes (.) But actually ask the people themselves.
   c) Да, в основном да. А вообще-то спросите у ребят самих
   [PAN TO AUDIENCE SMILES]

14a) D: Yes?

15a) Sov. Female A (trans.): You talk as though everybody here was
   b) # You talk as if everyone present here is
   c) Вы так говорите как будто бы вот каждый из пресутствующих

16a) already involved in that . I think when most of my girlfriends had
   b) doing it. I don't know about that, most of my girlfriends
   c) этим занимается. Я не знаю , большенство моих подруг

17a) gotten married at 18 or 20, they were virgins,
   b) got married when they were 18 and 20, and they all were virgins. # (.)
   c) вышли замуж в 18 и 20 они были девушками.

18a) and before marriage they did not engage in sex.
   b) # Before marriage did not even plan on having sex or sexual life.

c) До брака и вообще не собирались заниматься сексом и сексуальной жизнью.

19a) They were waiting for that one special man, for that one special
b) They were waiting for their one # (.) and only (.)
c) Они ждали своего одного единственного

20a) person, and they found that one special person.
b) #marriage with one person # (.) and they found it.
c) брака с одним человеком, и они его нашли.

21a) And most of their husbands also, for most of them their wife
b) And for the majority of their husbands (.)
c) И для большенства их мужей

22a) also was the first woman with whom they had ever had sexual relations.
b) as well (.) for them their wife was their first girl. (.)
c) тоже для них их жена была первая девушка.

23a)·
b) Woman that they liked.
c) Женщина которая понравилась.

24a) D: Is it true with most girls, most young women are virgins when
25a) they get married in the Soviet Union?

26a) SFA (trans.): Well, a great number of girls are virgins until marriage.
b) Well, (.) in general, (.) the larger part of girls are virgins before marriage. They just start leading that type of life after marriage.
c) Ну, ну в общем большая часть девушек является девушками до замужества. Они начинают только жить такой жизнью только после замужества.

27a) I don't really know, maybe not everybody.
b) Well, I don't know, maybe not (all/quite).
c) Ну я не знаю может быть не (все/совсем)

28a) Sov. Female B (trans.): You know, I just want to say
b) #I want to say
c) Я хочу сказать,

29a) that I think it's quite the opposite. You can't really say that it's
b) on the contrary# well in my opinion if not to say that it is
c) что наоборот, ну по-моему если не

30a) very good if a girl when she gets married is still a virgin, because
b) negative (.) you definitely cannot say that it is very good, if the girl when getting married is still a virgin (.)
c) отрицательное , то нельзя сказать что это очень хорошо если девушка выходя замуж еще девушка.

31a) I think quite the opposite. She should be quite sure
b) #Because I think that by that time, she basically should be sure
c) Потому что я считаю, тогда она вобщем-то уже должна быть уверенна

32a) of what her husband is as a man, that he'll be a real partner
b) of her husband as a man # (.)
c) в своем муже как мужчине

(continued on next page)

33a) for her, otherwise it could be a real tragedy.
   b) because otherwise it could be a tragedy. #(....................) #
   c) а иначе же может быть трагедия а иначе может быть трагедия (.......)

34a) And sex for a married couple is extremely important.
   b) It is very important # (....................) #
   c) Это очень важно(...............)

35a) After all, sex is 80% of happiness for a married couple
   b) Practically (.) makes up, #well, 80% of happiness.
   c) Практически, ну 80 % счастья занимает.

36a) but, of course, that depends on each individual woman.
   b) Of course it depends on every individual woman #
   c) **Естественно это зависит от каждой женщины**

37a) But for me I think that's very important.
   b) (....................)
   c) (....................)

38a) Sov. Female C : I think it is necessary to change the subject
39a) of conversation, because these questions are very deep
40a) to be concerned by us.

[AUDIENCE APPLAUSE]

41a) D (speaking over tape): This is day two of our visit to the Soviet
42a) Union. In this hour Soviet teens give a powerful exchange on
43a) everything from religion to war. But unlike American teenagers,
44a) areas they were reluctant to discuss included dating,
45a) school and sexuality.

46a) Sov. Male B (trans.) (in response to an inaudible question by Donahue): It's
   not a surprise that American students can't
   b) (....................)
   c) (........................)

47a) understand us, because they have many more problems
   b) Much more serious problems than (.) ours because (....................)
   c) На много серьезнее проблемы чем у нас потому что (............)

48a) than we have, the criminality, drugs, etc. Secondly,
   b) (....................) Secondly (.)
   c) (............) во вторых

49a) all boys and girls here are in somewhat different surroundings.
   b) all the young people here (.) found themselves (.) well, in (....................)
   c) все ребята сидящие здесь попали ну в (............)

50a) This is new to them. They've never been on television
   b) (....................) situation. (....................)
   c) (............) ситуации (...........)

51a) and this is the reason why they can't immediately talk to you

b) (...................)
c) (..............)

52a) as they do in America, where they are probably more easy going,
  b) We are not used to (*hanging out*) more uptight (....................) not
  c) Мы не привыкли (*шагаться*) скованней (................) не вероятно,

53a) and when they may even have experience of being on television.
  b) that they (*have ever been on television*).
  c) что они (*когда-нибудь были на телевиденье*)

54a) Sov. Male C (trans.): What can we do if everything is all right here?
  b) Well, what can we do if everything is all right? (.)
  c) Ну что мы можем сделать если все в порядке?

55a) Should we create problems?
  b) Should we think up a problem?
  c) Что, проблему придумать?

56a) Sov. Male D (trans.): We don't want to invent problems. Why?
  b) We don't want to invent ourselves the problems. Why?
  c) Мы не хотим придумывать себе проблем. Зачем?

   [LAUGHTER AND APPLAUSE]

57a) Sov. Male E: School is likewise, sometimes you are happy
58a) and sometimes you express just no particular emotions,
59a) and that's all.

60a) D: All right, I will listen to your advice and I will change the
61a) subject.

created through the means of public discourse. Donahue presumes his interlocutors can be influenced by televised discourse and thus can subsequently become "mediators of change,"[12] equipped (or informed?) better to redress these presumed imperfections. Donahue, then, attempts to co-create with his audience a kind of ritualized and rhetorical action, to display what he considers to be "a fitting response to a situation that needs and invites it."[13] The exigence (e.g., the unwanted pregnancies), the means of responding (e.g., public discourse, confessions, truth sayings), and its meanings (e.g., the remedy of a societal impropriety through public participation) all cohere from this view. Together, they provide a common and productive way to address social problems through open, public discussion, that is, by engaging in an American communication ritual. Donahue's interrogative utterances, as such, are not just journalistic questions or directives; they are moves in a culturally expressive—albeit ritually performed—game.[14]

The ritualized speech that Donahue presumes and initiates, how-ever, from the standpoint of the Russian expressive order, is inappro-priate, even incoherent. Immediately at lines 2 through 4, Donahue's interlocutor is taken aback (i.e., literally steps back from Donahue) while others laugh out loud, smile broadly, and whisper in each other's ears. The exigence Donahue invites his audience to address (e.g., the unwanted pregnancies) becomes immediately supplanted by another of their own (i.e., the foreign talk show host's unusual conduct). This imperfection grows with mounting urgency until finally, on lines 38 through 40, a woman speaks in English, the first audience member to do so, and tells Donahue, to the delighted applause of her "contempo-raries,"[15] that "it is necessary to change the subject," which Donahue eventually on lines 60–61 agrees to do.

An American Discursive Code

Note the question by Donahue in line 2: "You had sex when you were 18 years old?" He probes the issue by asking further about "contraceptive use" (line 4) and who took "care of this matter" (line 6), "protecting the girl from pregnancy" (lines 11–12). What exotic American tree is planted here, but later uprooted from Russian soil? What must be pre-sumed for these comments indeed to be intelligible?

Donahue's speech characterizes a kind of human activity, presum-ably coitus, as "had sex" and "practiced sex"; refers to it as an activity which is "practiced," then associates this "practice" with a technique, the "use" [of] a "contraceptive"; probes which individual was responsi-ble for its "use"; and mentions a biological motive for contraception ("protection from pregnancy"). Human procreative activity is commu-nicated here, then, as "sex," as an experience one "has" or "practices" in a particular way, which involves as part of the practice the possibility of contraceptive use, with this use being a primary responsibility of one of the involved individuals, because "protection" from deleterious biological consequences is desirable or necessary. The symbolic struc-turing of the topic invoked by Donahue thus draws attention—and di-rects subsequent discussion—to at least three prominent American cultural domains: physical facts (who did this activity, at what age, and with what biological consequences), technical utilities (what tech-niques or technologies were used), and individual actions (did *you*, in the singular, do it, who is responsible). The tone used for the discus-sion could be characterized as a "serious rationality," which fore-grounds not the passionate bonds among persons nor their moral status, but "sex" as a factual, technical, "practice" among individuals.[16]

Note further the sequence of symbols used, from "sex" (lines 2, 4) to protection from "pregnancy" (lines 11–12). The symbolic sequence takes "sex" in the direction of a problem of unwanted pregnancy and brings closer to the interactional surface other projectable problems that are culturally associated with this, problems such as premarital sex, irresponsible sexual practices, single-parent families, abortion, venereal diseases, AIDS, issues of morality, welfare systems, the population explosion, and so on. To an American ear, socialized within and exposed to such a system, all of this could come to pass rather naturally. One can hear, without too much strain or reflection, even if angered by this line of questioning, the kind of thing Donahue is getting at.

This line of questioning demonstrates a kind of "problem talk," or self-help dialogue, which functions—in part—to foreground various imperfections and thus to motivate subsequent utterances. The communicative form, a round-the-rally of problems-responses, typically involves a three-part spiraling sequence, which introduces a topic, renders it problematic, thus precipitating further responses that redress or elaborate upon the problems.[17] Note how the form takes a topic in the direction of problems, thus creating an exigence for various additional responses. The form—when animating American public discourse—creates outcomes in two directions: concerning the topics of discussion, it problematizes them, directing interlocutors along a plaintive conversation of flaws; concerning the form of public discussion, it motivates a spiraling of utterances that legitimates lengthy public discussion of the topic at hand. The form underlies much American public discussion, from talk shows to self-help groups to faculty meetings, leading those familiar with it to identify in it a kind of integrative communal action in which problems are discussed (not solved), relationships among those present being supported (or perhaps even strained). In popular American terms: "Here's the topic, it's problematic, we need to talk." On some occasions, this is a ritualized way of being American together.

Hearing Donahue as one engaged in this culturally expressive practice, then, leads us to hear that one might discuss this topic (i.e., coitus) in public, that it might be called "sex," that it might be symbolically constituted as a physical, technical, individual activity, that facts about it might be discussed rationally and seriously, that it is discussed and discussable as problematic. All of this is at least intelligible (if not entirely acceptable) to an American audience. The cultural game Donahue plays implicates a belief about "problem" talk: It is a potent social activity, an efficacious remedy for important social problems (which motivates a communally sensed urgency to the whole performance, once again).

The presupposed sequence—topic initiation, problematize, response cycle—as a general cultural form, invokes four common ground rules for speaking, with each containing culturally loaded symbols (in quotes): (a) In some American conversations, the presentation of "self" is a preferred communication activity, with statements of personal experiences, thoughts and feelings counting as proper "self" presentations; (b) Interlocutors must grant speakers the moral "right" to present "self" through personal statements; (c) The presentation of "self" should be "respected," that is, tolerated as a rightful expression; (d) Corporate and global (i.e., collective) standards are dispreferred because they unduly constrain "self," infringe upon inalienable "rights," and violate a code of personal "respect." These rules enable a public sense of free expression, a sacred grounding of the communal identity, "self," but they also create—necessarily—dissonance on topics and systematic refracting of such things as consensual truths, or collective standards of and for public judgment.[18] The *expressive order,* the form and rules, implicates and affirms a model of and for being a person: The person is deemed, first and foremost, "an individual" with a "self." As when one asks about "sex," or who is "responsible for contraceptive use," a belief is displayed about persons such that experiences and feelings are deemed unique, and culpability of agency is located with each. Affirmed in such a system is a powerful equivocal belief in both the separateness of each person (each person is a unique individual with freedoms and rights) and the common humanity for all (every person is at base an individual). Each and every "individual" can and must make "choices" such as whether to "have sex" or "use a contraceptive." Using these symbols in this way creates beliefs about a cultural person who has (or should have) "power" and "control" over the (societal/personal) "environment," but also because of this, the "individual" is the locus of responsibility and bears the greatest burden of and articulation in social life.[19]

These beliefs about the person are associated with the beliefs about talk and implicate a system of deep, cultural premises:

> *The person has two main parts,*
> *the physical (body), and within it*
> *the nonmaterial (thought & feeling)*
> *the nonmaterial cannot be seen*
> *it is a part of an inner world*
> *things are not part of that world*
> *other people can't know what things happen in that part*
> *speaking makes these things known to others*
> *and is a preferred action.*

These premises create a cultural notion of person that includes a body and its "mindful" part, the nonmaterial seat of personal being, which easily becomes the cultural site of discursive action and feeling.[20]

Turning back to our utterance, then, by Donahue on line 2, he is asking for a factual disclosure (confession?) about a Russian male's "individual self" (not the public's collective morality), about his physical experiences on an issue deemed publicly important and problematic. In so asking, he creates a cultural discursive space into which he expects his interlocutor to move. His hope is to create, with his Russian interlocutors, a ritualized—albeit popular American—public discussion. So designed, it is presumed that each person—as a "self"—can (and should) rationally discuss his or her own experience, thoughts, and feelings, display a serious rationality about "sex," thereby help to remedy the difficult exigence, the presumed "problems" with the Russian person and "society." These meanings, or something like them, must be hearable for his speech to make sense. With them, we hear a culture at work, on this intercultural occasion.

In Reply: A Russian Discursive Code

Immediately on hearing Donahue's first question, the largely Russian audience is aroused. Eyebrows are raised, laughter ensues, torsos wave back and forth with startled glances exchanged. At one level, and following the corrective action taken by the Soviet woman on lines 38 through 40, we might explain much by positing the rule: In public discussions, especially with outsiders, it is not preferable (even though possible) to discuss sexual matters. It is this moral proscription, evidently, that Donahue has violated with his line of questioning (lines 1–2, 6–7, 11–12), thus precipitating the previously mentioned reactions. The rule also accounts for some of the expressed embarrassment and reserve by the two women who spoke. As Donahue notes in his talkover (line 44), "They were reluctant to discuss." For an American ear, we hear through his phrasing an implication that "Something fishy is going on," perhaps more evidence of a "closed society," people unable, perhaps even constrained by the state, to speak their mind. But as stated, we have a negative, a general moral proscription, a how *not* to speak. What, then, is affirmed? What communication, from the standpoint of the Russian expressive order, should be forthcoming? And what does it instantiate that is cultural? What does it say about persons, social relations, talk, and feeling?

At this point the justifications offered by the males on lines 46 through 59 help orient our interpretation. Note the utterances take on an agonistic form, a contrasting of "your" American with "our" Russian ways. A comment made consistently and recurrently throughout the dialogues appears on lines 46–47: You Americans "can't understand us." Although several reasons are given elsewhere by the Russians for this (e.g., a biased and uninformed American media, poorly educated about Russian culture and history), the ones expressing the difference here are, you "have many more problems than we have, the criminality, drugs, etc." and Americans are accustomed to "being on television" and talking a certain way, but we (Russians) are not. What is amplified and applauded, to the delight of the audience, is this: "What can we do if everything is all right here? Should we create problems? We don't want to invent problems. Why?"

These Russian speakers have heard Donahue plodding down a problem-strewn path, which to them is incoherent—thus laughable—in this public context. "Should we create problems" just so we have something to talk with you about? There are at least two Russian premises supporting this question. First, we do not have these problems of premarital sex, drugs, and criminality. They are not parts of our lives. Indeed, during some interviewing, this position was asserted as an actual truth. Such things are said not to be part of the informants' everyday lives: "We don't hear about these things in our press, and we don't live with these kinds of people [drug users, criminals]. Sure, it might exist somewhere, but it's not part of my life, in my community." Given this as an uncontested discursive fact, then indeed "problems" such as these—at least for the immediate interactional moment—are ruled out of social existence.

Placing this Russian social fact alongside the American premise of "problems" precipitates replies by Americans of disbelief and skepticism. Thus, Donahue's talkover mentions a "reluctance to discuss" (line 44), "reluctance" implying that "they" are holding back the presumed truth about their problems, rather than "coming out" and stating this truth. Again, "reluctance" here becomes an American code word, which simply reasserts the Americanized "problem" focus and preferences for publicly personal self-talk about facts, translating the matter again into American terms and premises.

A second premise for the Russian line, "everything is all right here ... we don't want to invent problems" (lines 54, 56), orients less to facts and truth than to a proper stance for public conduct. The stance introduces the affirmative side of a rule system, a norm for proper comportment: In public discussion, especially with outsiders, it is preferable to speak a unified, corporate voice with statements of common morals and shared virtues counting as unifying. Given this rule, it becomes easier to hear how the first 37 lines of the segment are highly unusual for the Russian participants. Why would anyone come here and start talking first of all about private matters like "sex," and further, if that topic, about "problems" like premarital pregnancies?[21]

The Russian form for proper discussion, then, follows not an American sequence of topic initiation, problem statement, and response, but another in which a public topic, when socially ratified, is predicated to a collective agent through common virtues. Looking back to our segment from the standpoint of this Russian form, we can now hear, from the first speaker (lines 3, 5, 8 through 10, 13) to the second (lines 15 through 23), how discussion moved from the less virtuous, personalized, and factual, "I started [sex at 18]," to the more virtuous, collectivized, and moral "most/they/the majority were virgins before marriage." We also have an account for how the second Russian female speaker (lines 28 through 37) (called "courageous" by one Russian informant, a "Bimbo" by another) dared reveal an individualized (Westernized?) moral, "[before marrying him] a woman should be quite sure of what her husband is as a man." In so doing, she contributed to a sense of violation of the mentioned Russian rule because her statement was an individual opinion about a moral issue rather than a collective belief about shared virtues. This intensified the mounting sense of imperfection and urgency (i.e., more personal and public talk about sex), which immediately precipitated the corrective action on the next lines 38 through 40.

Russian dimensions of meaning ground the rules and form, and need to be highlighted. Note how the Russian rules require a clear division between public and private life, and distinguish the kind of talk proper in private among "insiders" from that which is proper in public for the sake of "outsiders," especially for "outsiders" who are sensed to be "officials of the [Soviet–Russian and American] state," as Donahue was keenly sensed to be.[22] This became quite pronounced when Donahue tried to interview Refuseniks, who would not talk with Donahue because they believed he was "cavorting" (*blat* or connected) with the "state." Donahue, being the free-standing individual he sensed himself to be, kept expressing utter bewilderment: "You appear to be upset with me, and I don't understand why." His reply, to "being a puppet in the state's hands," was "I'm controlling this!"[23] For our purposes, we simply use the moment to demonstrate how the Russian conversation, when deemed public or for outsiders, expresses a virtuous, connected collective. When matters turn private, for insiders, more individualized themes can prevail.

Listening with these rules, the form, and dimensions, one begins to hear in this talk a particular Russian sense, and with it to discover the various interactional sources of Donahue's breach. Here he brings to a public, collective forum, where shared virtues guide discussion, a private matter, which he explores through personal, individual, and scientific or factual terms. The exigence he unwittingly creates, or the "precipitating event," as Goffman called it, includes a configuration of at least these features: An improper topic (sex rather than the common morality of public life) is brought to a setting and discussed in an improper way (scientifically rational, technical, and individual rather than moral, passionate, and corporate) through an improper form (foregrounding societal problems rather than shared virtues). That Russians should act according to their own cultural forms and norms was made even more apparent to me during a meeting with a Russian student in my office. While discussing the public–private distinction in Russian social life, and seeing pictures of my children and wife rather hidden behind books and papers, I was asked: "Why make your family pictures available? You devalue your family and experiences and memories by doing this." And further, with regard to the topic of "sex" and related matters: "We don't discuss our personal experiences whatever they are [in public], love, sex, relations with God. We cannot express these in words. You make it shallow if you speak it in public." As one underground artist put it: "The most interesting things are going on in private where you can't see them." Here, then, we hear elaborated another feature: Public expression involves collective sayings which, relative to the individual/private, are shallow.[24] Private expression involves more intensely passionate sayings which are, as the woman in lines 30 through 40 put it, "very deep to be concerned by us." Private discourse among insiders runs deeper and involves greater volubility. Russian beliefs about public talk, then, orient to shared moral bases of life, and distinguish a kind of reserve in public with outsiders, from a greater expressiveness in private among insiders.

Our interpretation here can be extended by recourse to a central Russian cultural symbol, *dusa* (roughly, soul), which the Soviet[25] woman's phrase, "very deep," and the aforementioned dimensions culturally invoke. The beliefs about the person associated with this cultural symbol and elaborated with this expressive system create, like the American system, a persona of two parts, but the deeply felt, focal symbolic site of being differs:[26]

The person has two main parts
the body and the soul
one cannot see but one can feel the soul
because of the soul, things can happen in and among persons
that cannot happen in anything other than persons
these things can be good or bad
because of this part, a person can feel things
that nothing other than persons can feel.

This symbolically constructed notion of the Russian person entitles a dynamic integrative world that is "above all, emotional," morally colored, and holds strong transcendental overtones.[27] *Dusa* symbolically constructs a model person, then, not just as a distinct physical body with a rational and mindful self within, but further contrasts this organismic entity with a kind of cosmological connectedness, a transcendent moral realm (good or bad), a site of deep feeling that is distinctly interhuman. The desired locus of discourse, when forthcoming in public or in private, is not so much a rational, scientifically technical, individual utility as it is a passionate, morally connected, shared feeling.[28] As Pasternak put it in *Doctor Zhivago,* "You in others, that's what your soul [*dusa*] is."[29] Preferred Russian sayings usher forth, at least generally and characteristically, as soul-felt and relational expressions more than individually mindful and factual disclosures.

The Russian form for public discussion, conversational rules, and premises of personhood thus place us in a better position to hear this intercultural segment, especially the topic of "sex." Note that, for Russians, the concept "sex" entitles an activity that is more in the physical and animalistic domain than it is in the distinctively inter-human. As such, it violates the Russian sense of "soul," for the deeper soul of the person can and should involve only those things that can happen among persons. As one Russian woman put it: "Sex is something animals do." To discuss this topic in a factual, rational, scientific way, with regard to contraceptive techniques and "practices," in public terms of "animalistic mechanics," rather than in a proper moral tone of deep feeling that weds it with a common morality, and with uniquely human sensual passion, all of this is rather incoherent, even immoral, thus laughable within a Russian discourse. It is easier to see, then, how a Russian female, on viewing the segment, discussed how the first male speaker was put in the position of being a "fool and jerk," for he was swept into more rational/factual disclosures of individual, personally problematic, and animalistic experiences with "sex." The proper tone, form, and meanings, matters of the soul, virtuous positions, and unified themes were being wholly supplanted and elided.

SOUL AND SELF IN CONVERSATION

Russian conversation, as Russian life generally, is conducted through three fundamental cultural dimensions. The primary one is the keenly sensed difference between public and private contexts, with two respective others, shallow/deep and taciturn/voluble. Along these and other axes, discourse becomes public when outsiders or an outside influence is deemed present, precipitating rather taciturn sayings of relatively shallow, if collective, virtues. Created in the process is the rather famous Soviet public "front," the requisite "official Russia," Pravda's Russia, a conversational *pokazukha* or show.[30] Private contexts, on the other hand, are created primarily with insiders (e.g., kin and like ethnicity), framing speech as possibly going much deeper, as a context into which the passionate and sentimental dimension of lives are given a voice through what is called a "broad spirited" (*shirokaya dusha*), heart-to-heart or soul-to-soul (*po dusham*) kind of exchange.[31] The intensity, frequency, and durability of this relatively deep privatized expressiveness led one student of Russian culture to write of a "nation of incurable romantics," but also to contrast this with the cold, stuffy, pompous persona performed in public.[32] Conversational and cultural life in Russia apparently presumes and recreates such axes, contrasting a publicly shallow and taciturn face or "front" for outsiders with another more private, deep and voluble for insiders. As a public medium, television assumes these cultural bases for conduct and interpretation in Russia.

This cultural framing of televised talk in action reflexively constructs a dual quality in the Russian person. As a prominent observer of Russian life, Hedrick Smith, put it:

> *From childhood onward, Russians acquire an acute sense of*
> *place and propriety.... They divide their existence into*
> *their public lives and their private lives, and distinguish*
> *between "official" relationships and personal*
> *relationships.... They adopt two very different codes of*
> *behavior for their two lives—in one, they are taciturn,*
> *hypocritical, careful, cagey, passive; in the other, they*
> *are voluble, honest, direct, open, passionate. In one,*
> *thoughts and feelings are held in check.... In the other,*
> *emotions flow warmly, without moderation.*
>
> —Smith, 1976, pp. 135–148

The "soul" (*dusa*) of the Russian person, as a passionate, morally committed, distinctly human agent, and as the shared locus of communal symbolic life, is presupposed for each discursive performance, and is perhaps more happily and intensely elaborated in private. Given these beliefs about the medium, about conversation and the person, one can hear in such conversation its prominent symbolic motive and meanings: Express the "soul" of persons, human passion and morality, the good and the bad, in its dually distinctive, ritually performed, public and private ways.

American conversation, at least that part of it initiated by Donahue in this segment, is prominently motivated on the basis of an alternate view: Express your "self" honestly, with private experiences and personal opinions becoming easily elaborated as the context for public discussion. "Self" as something uniquely within, as something communally valued, and as something implicating the dignity both of that individual and implicitly of the person so conceived, becomes a public symbolic scene. Who is this unique person? What does one, as such, have to say? Informing others of one's own experiences, thoughts, and feelings, one's true and authentic self, the personal facts of the matter, becomes a prominent motive and context for public discursive action.

These interpretations offer several initial substantive findings with regard to Russian and American patterns of conversation, with each distinctive in its ritualized form. We find, on one hand, a soulful collective conversing on the basis of morality, orienting to the possible virtues of societal life. On the other hand, we find mindful individuals conversing on the basis of factual information, disclosing their real personal experiences in response to societal problems and issues. The former might sense the latter, at times as "soulless" (lacking morality, commitment, and loyalty to the common good), just as the latter might sense the former as "mindless" (lacking factual information and analytic abilities). These statements are of course generalities, characterizations of two distinctive cultural discourses, but they capture some of the conversational and cultural bases in this mediated conduct, and they identify some of the sources whereby each conceives of and evaluates the other. This general reading, built as it is around the cultural persona of each, is erected on the particular televised dynamics just detailed.[33]

Beyond these substantive findings, I hope this chapter demonstrates how a cultural discourse theory of media and audiences can be erected on the social and cultural foundations that people presume when they converse, and communicate generally. In this case, what is suggested is that Russians may see and hear this television text as a channel through which only certain things can (or should) be accomplished. Because it is a public text, conducted with and shown for "outsiders," it is a place for themes that are, relative to Americans, shallow and reserved. That Russian themes of morality and propriety are countered by American themes of efficiency, openness, and freedom for the "same" mediated text, should not escape our notice. Nor should all such cultural variations in the nature and social uses of the various media. Further, I hope these analyses suggest an ethnographic version of audience research. Erecting media theory on social and cultural foundations, and conducting our studies in this general way, should lead to some productive insights into the media, the messages of TV, and the expressive systems in which they have their basic, practical residence.

At play here are some of the possibilities of communication and culture theory for studying selves, expressive practices, and the media.[34] By drawing attention to an intercultural moment of self-presentations, brought to the fore are culturally diverse dynamics that are dense with meaning.[35] Exploring this moment has suggested certain modifications to the general theories of ritual and social drama through which cultural persona are being expressed, and viewed here.[36] In this conversational segment, we have heard how the sacred symbols of "soul" and "self" are active. Summarizing cultural beliefs about the person and mediated communication through key sacred symbols as these is risky, however. This might suggest a singular entity, a reified "thing," or unitary whole, a central or core symbol standing alone, somehow above or apart from a cultural communication system. But can one sever a part from the whole? I think not. Instead, one begins hearing distinctive expressive systems at work in singular utterances in sequence. One travels through the local discursive terrain to know each verbal ecosystem and the specific species of symbol that sets it apart. So we come to see, and hear, in the ritualized and dramatic sequences, cultural systems being asserted and reasserted, and symbolic meanings being acted. The eventual outcome is the replacement of an American "self" with a Russian "soul," a symbolic shift from the unique and honest one to the collectively compassionate moral locus of all. But the cultural force of this symbolic transformation can only be deeply displayed (if this is at all possible) by tracing the relevant radiants of meaning throughout each expressive system. In so doing, we find the ritualized drama motivated by such things as cultural dimensions (private/public, shallow/deep, taciturn/voluble), cultural forms for expression (proper topic, moral comment), and conversational rules (dispreferring beastial topics and preferring public displays of a moral voice); that is, the cultural discursive coding of an identity (an emotional, morally colored, and transcendent person). In this sense, the ritualized renewal of the Russian expressive order reinstitutes a core and sacred symbol, as it also supplants an American one. This happens however rather metonymically, for example, by making a change of topic, a shift in the cultural frame for the conversation. And thus cultural selves view and verbalize their lives on television, sometimes in distinctively ritualized forms, such that within this single conversation one seeks facts while another speaks morality. To know how this is so, we must hear in conversation not only generic sequences and forms, but with them cultural beliefs about persons and conversations.

ACKNOWLEDGMENTS

Parts of this chapter were originally published in the *Quarterly Journal of Speech*, (1993) 79, 182–200, in T. Lindlof & D. Grodin (Eds.), *Constructing Self in a Mediated World* (pp. 84–106), (1996), Thousand Oaks, CA: Sage, and translated into Russian in A. Pavlovskaya

(Ed. and Trans.), *Russia and the West: Dialogue of Cultures* (pp. 165–183), (1996), Moscow: Russian Academy of Sciences. Earlier versions of this chapter were presented as a Public Lecture at the New University, Lisbon, Portugal, December, 1990; at the Social Psychology Forum of Linacre College, University of Oxford, England, November, 1990; at the conference sponsored by the State University of New York, Albany, February, 1990; at colloquia at the Department of Communication, Arizona State University, December, 1989, and April, 1990; as a Public Lecture at the University of Tampere, Finland, in November, 1992; at the inaugural Communication Colloquium at the University of Haifa, Israel, May, 1993; at Hebrew University, Israel, May, 1993. Parts also have been discussed in detail at Moscow State University's Conference on Dialogue of Cultures in October of 1998, and other places since. The author would like to thank in particular Nelson Traquina, Rom Harre, Robert Sanders, Charles Bantz, Liisa Lofman, Tamar Katriel, Shoshana Blum-Kulka, Anna Pavlovskaya, Mikhail Makarov, Elena Khatskevich, among many others, for opportunities to discuss these ideas.

ENDNOTES

1. For a treatment of televised discourse as culturally coded see Donal Carbaugh (1988b, 1990b, 1996b, pp. 123–139); for other ethnographic analyses of mediated communication see Tamar Katriel (1991, pp. 93–122; 2004) and Gerry Philipsen (1992, pp. 43–61, 80–82, 87–98); for theoretical explications of communication codes and cultural communication see Gerry Philipsen (1997, 1987, respectively), Carbaugh (1995), and Carbaugh, Gibson, and Milburn (1995). For explorations of talk-show talk see Hutchby (1999), Priest (1995), Krause and Goering (1995), Manga (2003), Tolson (2001).
2. Throughout the essay, I use the term, *Soviet,* because that was the main term used by my informants and because the patterns I report were produced by speakers from various ethnic groups within the now dismantled Soviet Union. The term is of course not without its difficulties. I switch to the term, *Russian,* when the analysis suggests a distinctly Russian feature. Following standard usage, *American* refers to practices prominent and distinctive within the United States.
3. The ethnographic approach derives from Dell Hymes (1972), with recent formulations in Philipsen (1987, 1990, 1997; and Carbaugh, 1990a, 1990b, 1995, 1996b).
4. See, for examples, Richard Bauman (1970), Jack Daniel and Geneva Smitherman (1976), Kristine Fitch (1991), Yousuf Griefat and Tamar Katriel (1989), Tamar Katriel and Aliza Shenhar (1990), Gerry Philipsen (1992), and Ronald Scollon and Suzanne Scollon (1981).

5. See William Gudykunst and Stella Ting-Toomey (1988, p. 231), and Wendy Leeds-Hurwitz (1990). Also see Carbaugh (1990a, 1990b, 1990c).

6. For uses of exemplars or instances in communication studies see Robert Hopper (1988) and Scott Jacobs (1988).

7. The transcript consists of numbered lines and three tiers, a, b, and c. The text spoken in English appears as line (a). When tier (a) is an untranslated utterance in English, it is unmarked (e.g., 2a). When tier (a) is a translation into English (provided by an on-air network translator) of an utterance spoken originally in Russian, it is marked (e.g., 5a: [trans]). The (b) tier of a line provides, whenever possible, a second English translation (by an independent, nonnetwork affiliated Russian speaker) of utterances spoken originally in Russian. This provides readers with a kind of cross check between the translation provided by a television network, and that provided by a relatively independent Russian speaking viewer. This translation (on tier b) was of course not broadcast. Tier (c) provides as far as was possible, transcriptions of the Russian that was spoken on this occasion. This was very difficult to retrieve because the spoken Russian was often inaudible "behind" the on-air English translation. More details about how this kind of transcribing was done appears elsewhere (Carbaugh, 1993b, note 8, pp. 198–199). The different typefaces emphasize the different tiers of transcription.

8. The ritual interchange is a kind of "aligning action," a practice that invokes culture in conduct. See Randall Stokes and John Hewitt (1976) and Brad Hall (1991).

9. Goffman (1967, pp. 5–45). Also see Bitzer (1968).

10. The transcriptions, translations, and interpretations of the Soviet communication system were produced in collaboration with Olga Beloded, Diane Chornenkaya, Lazlo Dienes, Joseph Lake, and Vicki Rubinshteyn, among others.

11. As Donahue might know, part of the unspoken consensus in urban Soviet common culture is that many women have multiple abortions, with numbers in the twenties and thirties being not uncommon. See Hedrick Smith (1976, pp. 187-191).

12. Bitzer (1968, p. 11).

13. Bitzer (1968, p. 2).

14. See Tamar Katriel and Gerry Philipsen (1981) and Carbaugh (1988b, pp. 153–176).

15. See Clifford Geertz (1973, pp. 365–366).

16. A similar introduction to the topic of "sex" was made by an American medical doctor on a college campus who was conducting a workshop on sex education and birth control. He began with, "Tonight we're going to talk about sex. We're here to talk about social things, not moral issues. Whether it's right or wrong, good or bad, you'll have to decide for yourself. We're just going to talk about sex." Reported in "Condoms, Spermicides? Dr. Abel Doesn't Blush," *Collegian* 13 May 1991, p. 3.

17. See Carbaugh (1988b, pp. 127–166).

18. Summary based on Carbaugh (1987).
19. Carbaugh (1988b, pp. 21–86); also see Carbaugh (1988/1989).
20. The premises formulated here and above are adapted from Anna Wierzbicka (1989) and her system of semantic primitives. See also Rom Harré (1984).
21. Extremely important to note is that the Soviets in this segment almost never use the term *sex* alone. Their discussion of this topic occurs in a rather veiled style. The four veiled references to this topic are as "it" (line 8), "that" (line 16), "that" (line 37), and "the subject" (line 38). At two points, the Soviet translators supply differing terms. At line 34, the network translator (line 34a) supplies "sex," while the independent translator (line 34b) supplies "it"; at line 35 the network translator (line 35a) supplies "sex," whereas the independent shows no translation of the term. Similarly, the veiled predications [with implications] about the topic are: "I started" [sexual life at age 18] (line 3); "I was well prepared" [for sexual life] (line 10); "sure of what her husbands is as a man, that he'll be a real partner" (lines 31a and 32a) or "be sure of her husband as a man" [adequate partner for sexual life] (lines 31b and 32b). One difference between translators occurs with regard to the relevant predications: "the first woman with whom they had ever had sexual relations" (line 22a) or "their wife was their first girl (.) woman that they liked" (lines 22b and 23b). Russian constructions of the topic are thus relatively veiled, oblique, or indirect (e.g.,"it" or "that"), as are predications about the topic (e.g., "be a real partner" or "woman that they liked").
22. See Smith (1976, pp. 6-7, 137-140).
23. See Smith (1976, p. 18) for the cultural (more than the political) roots that highlight the connected agent over "the individual." As one informant put it: "In the Russian culture, it is common to address issues of life from a global and moral perspective. Personal beliefs about social practices are presented as exercised patterns of behavior. They might be heard as more or less typical, but they are usually predicated to a collective agent. The speaker's views are supposed to be shared by a collective beneficent." The importance of designing speech with a collective and connected voice is evident also in a common Russian proverb told to schoolchildren: "I is the last letter in the alphabet," which means according to one informant, "put yourself after the others on your list of priorities." The same cultural principle creates the Soviet form of postal address, beginning at the top with the country of the addressee, under which comes their city name, then their street name, with the individual's name at the bottom, last name first.
24. See Smith (1976, p. 21).
25. Russian viewers of this segment guessed this woman was, in 1987, from a southern "Soviet" state, thus the reference to her as "Soviet."
26. The following formulation is adapted from Wierzbicka (1989).
27. Wierzbicka (1989, p. 52).
28. Realizing this helped me reflect upon what had been a very puzzling situation. A Russian student had called me at home one evening and

asked, with no explanation, the date of my birth. Later, I realized the student was making decisions about advisory committees and wanted to know my astrological sign as a way of interpreting the nature of our connection within a transcendentally connective, feeling-full domain. The inference I draw from this exchange is not of course that all Russians are astrologers, or actors on cosmic feeling. What the exchange displays, I think, is a communicative instance of a cultural orientation, which itself coheres activities in terms more passionate, transcendentally connected, and feeling-full, than does the American, centered as it is in terms of scientific rationality, expressive technicality, and individual utility.

29. Quotation taken from the Russian version; see Wierzbicka (1989, p. 54).

30. Analyses based on other data corroborate and extend the claims developed here. See Carbaugh (1990b, pp. 159–160, 1993a).

31. The precise ways the public/private dimension becomes interactionally operative is unclear, although "public" is apparently cued not solely on the basis of outside participants (like Donahue), but outside influences generally, including jazz. Hedrick Smith (1976) described how Moscow audiences responded with heightened intensity, great amounts of sobbing and laughing to Russian ballet, but when viewing American ballet, or jazz, were much more restrained and reserved.

32. Smith (1976, pp. 135–148, ff.).

33. The primary data for this report were gathered in 1987 through 1990, prior to the dismantling of the USSR. What effects these recent political developments may have on the patterns described here is currently unknown. For some informants, the patterns described here are very durable, even in the face of pressures to change. As one informant put it, "We don't know how to do it any other way," with "it" referring to their habitual patterns of expressive life. For the robustness and pervasiveness of traditional Russian styles, see Jane Kramer (1990). Whether these cultural dynamics apply more generally cannot be firmly asserted on the basis of this report. I can, however, add that I have witnessed the Soviet–Russian pattern identified here in many contexts in the United States, in Europe, and in Russia. Various readers of this report assure me they have observed these patterns in various places, including in Israel among Russian immigrants. Perhaps most gratifying have been reactions by Russians, various scholars of Russian culture and history, and Russian scholars themselves, the latter soliciting this essay repeatedly for publication in a Russian journal and other outlets. I mention this not to claim any final word in the matter—in fact I see what is here as only a beginning—but to suggest that this report, whatever its flaws, has struck at least some cultural chord. How broadly the Soviet and American patterns apply, and if so, how intercultural encounters between them display these patterns, to what extent these apply to vari-

ous contexts and media of communication, all of this warrants further study. See also Carbaugh 1993b, pp. 195–196.

34. See Michael Moerman (1988, pp. 104–107).
35. For the social drama frame see Victor Turner (1980).
36. See Victor Turner (1980), Gerry Philipsen (1987), and my related studies (Carbaugh, 1993a, 1993b, 1996b).

⊰⧚ 6 ⧚⊱

"I Can't Do That!" but I "Can Actually See Around Corners": American Indian Students and the Study of "Communication"

"I can't do that!" The young woman was talking to me in my office about a required speech to be delivered in a public speaking course. Her first assignment involved preparing and delivering a 5- to 7-minute speech that demonstrated a basic process or principle. We had been going over—in class and now again in my office—some of the possible tactics one might use to design and produce such a speech when her hands trembled, her eyes watered, and with her head bowed she exclaimed forcefully through clenched teeth, "I can't do that!"

Now, some years later, I remember vividly her highly intense emotional response. In fact, her reaction was so intense that I began immediately searching for possible reasons for her expressed difficulties, so I could help her. While it took years for me to eventually understand even some of her concerns, some of the meanings in her exclamation, "I can't do that," we nonetheless worked hard together, for hours, to prepare for the delivery of her first speech—which turned out to be a very painful event for everyone involved, especially her.

The young woman in this opening story is Mina Running Eagle, a member of the Blackfeet Indian Nation which is centered upon a reservation in northern Montana, in the United States.[1] Over the next semesters and years of my teaching, I had occasion to contact several Blackfeet students in communication classrooms. Not all, nor even most were like Mina, but in her actions, we can eventually hear parts of the Blackfeet culture at work. After giving some time to reading about the Blackfeet, making their acquaintance, and learning some of their ways through observing and being with them, I have come to a somewhat better understanding of Ms. Mina Running Eagle, and of what she was up against in her university course in public communication. Her exclamation of "I can't do that!" carries enduring meanings, and with the passage of time, has assumed newer meanings for me.

In this chapter, I seek to show how I came to some understanding of Mina's exclamation by exploring two sets of cultural premises for communication that surrounded this required university course. By reflecting in this chapter on this event, and similar others, I demonstrate a complexity of cultural features that are involved in these and similar communicative events, and thus suggest what reflecting on them can contribute to our critical understanding and practice of communication. I hope readers' teaching and understanding of communication will benefit, as mine has, by reflecting on the use of diverse cultural forms of communication in settings of education, and in other human institutions.

BLACKFEET "COMMUNICATION"[2]

My grandparents taught me: The people lived in harmony with nature. The animals were able to speak. Their understanding of communication was far more advanced than from today's standards.

—Rising Wolf

Some traditional Blackfeet people, like Rising Wolf, on some occasions, use a cultural model of "communication" that presumes, *sui generis*, a patterned way of living. A premise of this "communication," from the Blackfeet view, might be called a "deep attentiveness," a listener active form of nonverbal vigilance to all that is presumably interconnected. Rising Wolf, identified by tribal members as a Blackfeet "blood" (i.e., a full-blooded Blackfeet), introduced that form of communication to me as something he was taught by his grandparents, and discussed it further in this way: you are "able to communicate spiritually and physically … you are in tune with something long enough, to a point that you know it inside out." His main examples of this cultural form, of which there were many, consisted of detailed descriptions of "communicating with the animals," for "you had to be pure mind, pure thought in order to communicate with the animals." A goal of Blackfeet communication, according to Rising Wolf, is to "actually live that life … to live that life every day." In this Blackfeet sense, communication is less an event or style of verbal action, than it is a premise for all action, an active way of being in the world.

This Blackfeet view of communication involves the realization of a holistic belief, that people, animals, spirits, and things form an interrelated co-presence, a dynamic togetherness of which one is part and parcel, in which one dwells. This kind of realization is both an ideal for

communication that is especially apparent in some special Blackfeet
ceremonies (e.g., sweat-lodge rituals). It is also a desirable condition
for more routine, everyday communicative action. For this kind of
communication to be forceful in social living, it assumes (and thus creates) a watchful stance, an unspoken attentiveness to the interconnections that are known in a largely nonverbal and nonlinguistic way, yet
are shared and publicly accessible, if one just listens.

This cultural mode of communication creates a special significance
for nonlinguistic channels of messages, and an important duty for
communicants as listeners. Participants in this communication must
therefore become active and practiced *as* listeners, already exercised
as observers of that which they are already a part. In a conversation
with me, Rising Wolf described the considerable challenges of this
ever-watchful form of communication in this way:

> It's the hardest thing to concentrate on
>> what you really believe in
> It's the hardest thing
>> to listen
> It's one of the hardest things I think human beings have
>> is to listen
> And actually listen and hear what they listen to
>> not listen and then make up their own mind
>>> of what they heard
>> Which is pretty common today
> But to actually listen.
>> And you start hearing the spirits talking
>> And they communicate with people like Bigfoot, the eagle,
>>> elk, deer, the rocks, water
> When these spirits come in
>> you can feel, or
>> you can hear those spirits and
>> you can feel them doing things to you.
> Say if an eagle came in
>> you could feel the breeze of that wing as he flies by
>> you can feel it when he comes and puts his head by you
> Same with an animal that has hair
>> you can feel the hair
>> you can feel the difference in hair too
>>> if you're born in the mountains

been around mountains

been around animals

you've always touched the animals, so

you can tell the difference

you can close your eyes and

you can almost say

this is a dog

this is a deer

this is an elk

So you can tell that

in the ceremonies.

By going through those there

it rejuvenates your spiritual, spirituality

and your rebirth of your confidence in who you are

and that it's still alive and strong

and no matter how far back East in some city you might be

you know that nature and the communication

between the animals and man is still there.

it makes you feel spiritually strong

to the point that you just want

to jump with cheer and joy.

And you go back to your city life with that energy.

Rising Wolf's words point to a dimension of experience that is itself not a verbal event, but a real spiritual and physical event in which a person can (and should) participate. When engaged in this kind of communication, meanings of interconnected living are constantly being recreated, if one listens and observes properly. This is a most valued event, a scene presumed for and created in some traditional Blackfeet communication. Such a scene is sought and realized not primarily through verbal interaction, but through actively listening to all that is present.[3]

This form of communication can be alluded to with a rather quick verbal reference. A middle-aged Blackfeet male, Perry Weasel, invoked this cultural form of communication with these few words, as he told me about his grandfather: "He was a superb communicator," then later, "He very rarely verbally talked, but there was just always a sense of knowing. His communication had a great effect on me as a child." The grandfather embodied and taught "superb" Blackfeet communication, not mainly through the words he spoke, but with a nonlinguistic "sense of knowing."

Using—what I now understand to be—this mode of communication, a Blackfeet boy in my class on public communication, gave what one fellow student called a "mesmerizing" 7-minute public presentation (i.e., a "public speech"). This consisted of actively and artfully maneuvering the martial art tool, *nunchakus,* for his "speech." The only verbal portion of his speech consisted of only three words, "like an eagle," spoken once, about midway through his 7-minute presentation.

In these comments and actions, a primary and traditional mode of Blackfeet communication is being culturally invoked, and signified. It involves a kind of listener active, participant co-presence within shared activities, with each activity (e.g., Leon Rising Wolf's words, Perry Weasel's grandfather, the nonverbal speech) demonstrating a kind of Blackfeet communication. Through this mode, the Blackfeet are "saying" something about people being already connected (part of a holistic scene), about people, spirits, and ancestors being an inherent part of this grand picture, about natural features and animals being figured into this interconnected realm, with all of this providing a known, Blackfeet cultural scene. A primary mode of some Blackfeet communication is thus to "communicate spiritually and physically" through a listener-active attentiveness with a cultural premise (a belief and value) that this mode is an inheritance of a holistic world of intricate interconnections.

This means of communicative living is difficult for Blackfeet to sustain in some of, what they have called, "Whiteman's" educational settings, especially away from the reservation, yet it is also a means of coping with that very difficulty. As Rising Wolf put it:

After I finish school here
I go back [home, to the reservation]
    to regenerate my knowledge
    to regenerate my spiritual beliefs
        myself
By going to the sweats and start communicating again
    with the animals and the way of life around you
        the frustration, the turmoil, the confusion of everything
            is gone
Y'know, you've got a clear mind and a clean body
    you can think
    you can see a lot better
    you can actually see around corners
    you can actually feel things happen
        when they actually happen

So today I use my Indian ways to help me communicate

in the Whiteman's world

and travel through it.

Notice how Rising Wolf has structured his comments. For him, the "Whiteman's" "school" had created "frustration," "turmoil," and "confusion." When he was able to "start communicating again," in the Blackfeet way, he was able to "think," "see," and "feel" "a lot better," to the point that he could "see around corners." Through his Blackfeet ways, he was able to tune into the "way of life around" him, and let it speak to him. As a result, he was able both to "regenerate" his "knowledge" and "beliefs," and to "travel through" "the Whiteman's world."

For Blackfeet people who hold to, socially enact, and valorize this primary mode of connective co-presence, verbal speaking and speaking in public can assume a secondary status or importance. Yet to speak in public, literally to say words while in the presence of many others, is an important skill for some in the tribe to master (cf. Wieder & Pratt, 1990, 1993). In fact, speaking well is a valued art, as we see shortly (cf. Clements, 2002). But it can also be risky as a social action. Speaking in public is risky, for it can sever or tear the actual or presumed interconnections among people, and thus pollute the communal waters from which every member of the tribe draws sustenance. Part of the risk in speaking also results from stepping into a very weighty social position: It is to be one who can and should take such a performative risk; it is to be one who has been apprenticed in the proper form for this public, verbal action; it is to be one who is known by the community to be so apprenticed and so skilled; it is to be one whose speaking others can trust, for to speak is to carry (not necessarily only positive) repercussions for the community and the interconnected world. Speaking in public is thus to activate an important, though at times secondary, mode of communication that is risky as a form of social action and weighty as to its social position.

For traditional Blackfeet people, the social position associated with speaking in public is most typically, but not exclusively, an elder male.[4] As noted, to be one who can so speak is to be one of the proper social rank including one who has been tutored for years in proper public speaking. The risk of speaking, however, is magnified when in the presence of certain audience members, especially when with outsiders and elders. Jon Moore, a professional, highly educated (PhD) middle-aged Blackfeet male who "enjoys speaking to kids," discussed the special context created when older people are in his audience: "I don't like to talk in front of older people. Subconsciously, I get a feeling of inadequacy, not up to par with everyone else, fear that you might tread on waters you shouldn't tread on because you're not as experienced as someone in the crowd." To do so, for

Moore, presumes a place for yourself where you do not quite fully belong. Presumably, those best equipped to speak are those who have been a part of this world the longest, are properly "in tune" with it, and have been properly trained to speak about it. As another Blackfeet put it: "If you speak out, you subject yourself to criticism," with this criticism coming most likely from those deemed most knowledgeable and skilled at public speaking, the elders of the tribe.

To speak, then, implies that one is presuming a particular social position, but further, that one is conducting a weighty social action. Because the act itself involves pulling something out of the interconnected realm and giving it verbal attention. This is intrinsically a risky action, in that what one extricates from the interconnected realm is potentially (through the interconnective premise) a part of everyone's shared world, and that speaking about it invokes a knowledge that is often the special province of the elders. Speaking then presumes that one has stepped into a revered social position, that one has command of knowledge requisite to that social position, that one has the exercised ability to indeed speak about this in the presence of the present others, and that what one is verbalizing might—in varying degrees—be already known to everyone present.[5]

Those best equipped for public speaking are also those most socially knowledgeable (i.e., the elders). As an elder, one incurs the obligation to embody and transmit communal ways, and, when appropriate, to speak for other members of the community. This is an important ability because "speaking for others" in this way is a way of properly vocalizing the concerns of others in communal affairs. That Blackfeet are prominently members of the familial community is evident with the wide use of a popular form of address—*nixokoawa* [my relations]—which expresses this presumed collective membership, and indicates possible access of each to the others, including the elders who can speak for them. Important to emphasize here is that the elder, in the performance as a vocalizer for others, is speaking not just for himself or herself but is speaking carefully and artfully as a key member and representative of an already interrelated community. The basic premise for such speaking is the interrelated whole of which each is an integral part. The specific focal concern being expressed by the individual who is speaking thus plays the concerns of individuals within this largely familial and communal scene. Through this process of elders being vocalizers for and with others, all members of the Blackfeet tribe—including all others who are not elders—can be involved in communal, political, or tribal affairs, without having to publicly vocalize their concerns.[6]

These modes of Blackfeet "communication" rely on, and, in turn, recreate deeply held cultural values. Some of these are the nurturing of the tribal heritage and natural geography, which have been transmitted historically through tribal ancestors (especially grandparents), events (e.g., traditional encampments, sweat-lodge ceremonies), and the unspoken system of interconnections that precedes and encompasses any one sentient being, thing, or event. Related values involve modesty (deferring to the difference of each other, and a reverence for the whole) and stability (continuity of belief and value across time) with particular tribal members deemed a small and relatively unimportant part of this rather durable and holistic, spiritual and physical world. Within this communal scene, persons and relations are erected upon a valuing of, and respect for social difference, with the society, and public speaking itself being at times a performance of social differences based on individual autonomy, age, and gender.

In summary, then, Blackfeet "communication" can be understood through two modes of communication. The primary mode involves a nonverbal, listener-active, co-presence and its associated premise of interconnectedness. Figured upon this primary mode is a secondary mode, verbal speaking, which is deemed risky as a social action (because it might violate the presumed interconnectedness), and presumptuous as to social position (in that one steps into a highly respected position presuming one can so act by speaking). This secondary mode relies on and invokes social positions of difference with elders being the traditional public vocalizers. These modes of communication and the cultural life they express reflect a valuing of heritage, nature, modesty, stability, and respect for differences in social positions.

"WHITEMAN'S" COMMUNICATION

The alternate model of communication that Mina Running Eagle had contacted in her college course on public communication could be called a "Whiteman's" or "White people's" model, this being the way it is characterized by the Blackfeet. Note that here, with this cultural model, the primary mode of communication is not a listener-active co-presence, but verbal speaking. It is based at least partly on an alternate set of cultural premises: Speaking makes something public that was heretofore private, personal, or internal; Speaking helps create (or construct) social connections among those who were presumably different or separate; and, connecting through speech is the principal way a society is made, and made to work. From the "White people's" view, the primary mode of communication is verbal speaking, with this mode being important for the actual constructions of personal, social, and societal life (Cameron, 2000; Carbaugh, 1988b; Katriel & Philipsen, 1981; Philipsen, 1992). As "White" students in my classes have asked, after being introduced to some nonverbal ways of communicating, how do you communicate if you don't say anything?" In response, Blackfeet students, among others, look at each other and smile.

With speaking assigned a valued means of expression in "the White-man's" system, silence assumes a rather secondary role. Communicative silence can be figured on, or under the primary mode of verbal speaking. Silence thus can be played against the primary mode by risking its negation, or by signaling the absence of the very premises that are presumably activated when "White people" speak in a "White" way. Silence as a communicative action can mean, to "White people," a negation of one's personal being (as in "the silent treatment"), a failure to connect with others in relationship, and a sign that social institutions have been ruptured or broken or corrupted (e.g., "a conspiracy of silence"). Without speaking, in silence, one can hear (or feel) not an interconnectedness as among the Blackfeet, but an unhealthy separateness, and disconnectedness that is present between presumably different individuals or peoples. In this way, silence can be a prominent way to accentuate the different, separate, and even disconnected states of affairs, which are so often presumed as a basis for many public American (i.e., multicultural) events and scenes.

For the Anglo speaker, on public occasions, the primary mode of verbal speaking is typically associated not with a special role of "elder," but with the prominent and common social position of "citizen." Speaking in public, as a political and legal (i.e., constitutional) matter, is a performative possibility for everyone. The action of speaking in public is an essential part of being a citizen, with this action being cultivated in the nation's legal codes. As a citizen, one is entitled to "speak in public," and given this "right," one can (and should) exercise it—and permit it to be exercised—rather "freely." The role of "citizen," from the vantage point of this primary mode of speaking, then, is not erected fundamentally upon social differences between the members of the society, but is erected upon a political premise of commonality among all members of the nation of the United States of America.

Because speaking is available to all citizens, and because it can be used to construct personal lives and social organization, one can use speaking as a means both to gain access into society and to better one's place within that society. This Anglo belief—and the attendant, deeply felt necessities for construction and progress—it is crucial to recognize, is not a natural state of human beings, but is a belief that has been created, partly through this cultural conception of *speaking*. Further, it is being actively (re)created each time the political position of citizen is being connected with the primary expectation for verbal participation, and all of the typical cultural premises associated with that expectation (i.e., verbal participation as the necessary means of constructing, and bettering individual, social, and sociopolitical life). Some of the values associated with this belief system are upward mobility (that one can and should do better than one's current lot in life), change (that one should be different or "grow" beyond one's present state), and progress (that movement and change is necessary for betterment and improvement). These values can be often operationalized at a personal level, leading "the Whiteman" to articulate and assert, even demand the values of change and uniqueness (that individuals are psychologically different, and should aspire to become better and different as a person).

The "white person's communication," then, relies on a primary mode of oral speaking, with this being the means through which personal, social, and sociopolitical life is constructed. The secondary mode of silence can play upon this primary mode and thus can become a prominent way of signifying the absence or negation of the possibility for personal, social, and sociopolitical life. The quintessential social position associated with verbal speaking in public is the role of citizen, which is based on a common political model of "individual rights" among the nation's members. Anglo "communication," designed this way, reflects and creates beliefs about the separateness of individuals as well as the optimism of constructing a personal yet communal life, while valuing upward mobility, change, progress, and uniqueness.

INTERCULTURAL DYNAMICS IN THE CLASSROOM

With the benefit of these different cultural understandings of communication (see summary in Table 6.1), we might now better understand Mina Running Eagle's comments, and the larger situation in which she found herself. What was she saying, when she said, after being introduced to her course assignment, and after having it described in my office by me: "I can't do that!" What exactly was it that she could not do?

The general, "Whiteman's" logic of the classroom assignment to which Mina responded could be put this way: As a citizen of this country, you will be required to speak in public, and you yourself can benefit from so speaking. Thus, learning to speak in public is essential to your general liberal arts education. In this class, the first assignment requires you to speak for about 5 to 7 minutes. You will verbally inform the class about a topic (a basic process or principle) of your choice, one that is important to you, but also one that is important to this class, or this community today. In your speaking, you will not only display what you know about the topic, but also you will help construct a sense of that topic for your audience. This was the task before her.

From Mina's point-of-view, she had a different, or additional cultural frame-of-reference that competed for her allegiance, and with

TABLE 6.1
Summary of Blackfeet and "Whiteman's" Models of Communication in a Classroom Setting

	BLACKFEET	"WHITEMAN"
Primary Mode:	Silence →	Speaking →
Cultural Premise:	Listener-active Interconnected	Speaker-active, Constructive
Secondary Mode:	Verbal Speaking →	Silence →
Cultural Premise:	Risky, Rupture	Division
Social Position:	Differences by gender and age	Commonality, equality
Typical Speaker:	Elder Male	Citizen
Cultural Persona:	Relational Connection	Unique individual
Values:	Nature, heritage, modesty, stability	Upward mobility, change, progress

which she reacted to the assignment. Perhaps this, her interpretation, reflected—as another Blackfeet put it—a deeply subconscious, physical and spiritual worldview or ethos. From this, Mina's view, the assignment was creating a social position of public speaker, which was foreign to her and her place in her communal ways. Incoherent social expectations were being created for her as the assignment asked her, a young female adult, in effect, to speak publicly, and thus to step into the traditional position of being an elder male. With regard to the age dimension of this speaking role, she was too young and had no experience or training or at this point even desire to become an elder who would or could so speak. With regard to the gender dimension of this speaking role, she had of course no real physical or cultural experience. Public actions of speaking would (and should) come, if at all, much later in her developmental and cultural scheme of things. In effect, the course was addressing her as one who must perform in a social position that she respectfully reserved for elders, especially elder males.

With regard to her communication activities, she had been watching and "listening" carefully in class. She knew she was being asked to perform verbally (in her secondary mode), and she also knew that her verbal performance was to be witnessed by an audience that included two types of people—"Whitepeople," who were unfamiliar to her, including her male teacher—cultural persona that were culturally salient to her, and to whom she felt public speaking was deeply inappropriate. To speak to this public was, to her, both inappropriate and incredible. From her cultural frame of reference, this presented considerable problems, for she was being required to talk in public, to do so to people who were different and knew more than her, and further to do so in a scene which to her was very disconnected from her past, thus removing traditional sources of knowledge she had been taught to recognize, use, and value. Further, she was being asked to perform through a public communicative mode that was secondary to her. This kind of communication, itself, even for an elder male (like Jon Moore), is risky. To act this way, at so young an age, as a female, to this group of "Whitepeople," including a teacher, from whom she was culturally disconnected, all of this was nearly incomprehensible and anxiety provoking for her. As a middle-aged, very successful, highly educated, public male Blackfeet figure put it: "When I was younger, I used to get sick when I'd have to speak." Imagine how Mina felt.

We could summarize the sense of confusion and violation that the assignment created for Mina by formulating at least these two sets of conflicting, cultural messages: (a) About what was deemed proper in a learning environment: Mina was caught between Blackfeet demands to be a respectful attentive student and "the Whitepeople's" expectation that she be a verbally active student; (b) About what was deemed sensible as social organization: She was caught between her Blackfeet status as a young adult female and "Whitepeople's" expectations that treated her as a citizen, with this role of citizen placing her incredibly, from her Blackfeet view, in the position of a male elder; (c) About communication: She was caught between Blackfeet demands to silently attend to the primary, proper connective scene rather than the "Whitepeople's" expectations to exercise, what was to her, a secondary, presumptuous verbal performance; (d) About attitudes toward the audience: She was caught between her Blackfeet heritage that taught her to respect differences in people based on age and gender and thus remain observant, rather than enact the "Whitepeople's" citizen role and speak out; and (e) About the values that should be operative in this scene: Mina felt both the Blackfeet imperative to exercise proper modesty and respect for self, scene, and others, and the "Whitepeople's" apparent requirement to exercise a productive verbal efficacy. Because she was being asked (required) to be, what she considered to be, inappropriately verbally active, incredibly an elder spokesperson, improperly speaking to an audience she did not know but whom she knew included "Whitepeople," and a male teacher she wanted to respect, and because she thought the assignment required her to be not only rude but someone whom she was not and could not be, she exclaimed: "I can't do that!"

Beyond Mina's particular position, we could summarize the generally operative intercultural dynamics in this classroom in this way: In public speaking, "Whiteman's" model presumes a common role of citizen, and a primary mode of speaking, which is based on beliefs about the separateness of individuals and thus the necessity to verbally construct life. Such constructions are often guided by the values of upward mobility, change, and progress. From the Blackfeet point of view, setting the educational scene in this way puts undue emphasis on a secondary mode of communication (i.e., verbal activity), and strips the social scene of its deepest resources (i.e., physical and social interconnections), its proper persona (i.e., elders), and its most valued features (i.e., of heritage, modesty, and respect for differences in gender and age). Entirely supplanted in this scene is the more primary Blackfeet mode of traditional communication (which to "Whitepeople" can symbolize not affirmation and holism but negation and division) and the proper beliefs about persons, social positions, tribal living, and values associated with it.

CULTURALLY SITUATED, CRITICAL REFLECTIONS

In the contemporary world that we [Native Americans] deal with, we have an understanding of all the other religions, different types of language and cultures. Then when we try to communicate, say, with the people around us, or the people we're working with, it's really hard to do because [pause] of a lack of understanding of other Ind— of other people. Where a White person, wh— I don't know. [long pause] a confusion will really set in because White people don't understand the Native American.

—Rising Wolf

What is an ethnographer's responsibility when confronted with situations like these, as in some scenes of education when a female American Indian student exclaims, "I can't do that!"? Or, when a male American Indian student gives a 7-minute "speech" of three spoken words? Or, similarly, when Blackfeet males come to one's office to "speak for" a Blackfeet female?

I think we should, first of all, educate ourselves about such moments of communication, and be sure we recognize if, and when, and how, there are cultures at work in them. For each educational context, and for each peopled place, there will be cultural views of communication operating. Perhaps for some, a verbal channel is deemed valuable and very constructive; it is used as a way for each to exercise fundamental rights of each human being. Teaching and learning this channel is highly valued by them, for it can carry great force in their common political life. Failing to engage the verbal channel can lead, from this vantage point, to missed opportunities, continued oppression, even social disorganization. For others, from another view, a nonverbal channel is deemed valuable and connective; it is a way of inhabiting an already inhabited world. Teaching and learning this channel is highly valued, for it keeps one "in tune" with physical and spiritual life. Failing to learn and exercise the nonverbal channel can lead, as some Blackfeet have said, to "elimination," "confusion and turmoil." As teachers, researchers, and citizens, we should be vigilant and cautious when the former "White" view requires the Blackfeet to speak up verbally and be heard, even (especially?) under the guise of "participatory democracy," for the demand itself supplants the very goal it seeks to attain. From the other angle of vision, if the Blackfeet were to make a demand, it might be for us to watch and listen, to be respectful and modest of that which we are all a part, especially when in the presence of something to which we are not yet attuned, like a deep cultural difference. The latter suggestion seems forcefully pertinent today, because it is too often "talked over," especially when our expectations are built on narrow conceptions of "communication" and "democracy," with the accompanying imperative that all voices speak up and be heard.

Ethnographic studies of intercultural communication can help us understand how different cultural orientations relate to practices of living like these, in and out of the classroom. They can help us understand the complexity and depth of perplexity created in some intercultural encounters, as when one sees great value in speaking up, participating and being heard, whereas the other sees value in remaining quiet, for so much goes (and should go) without saying. Knowledge as this is necessary if we are to understand and critically reflect on intercultural relations of each with the other.

In situations of education like the ones between the "White" teacher and the Blackfeet students, we must get to know better what our students are doing when they communicate. We must know who we, as teachers, are teaching, and the depth (when there is depth) of what we, therefore, are dealing with as we teach. In the process, we can come to know better what we are doing as teachers, only as we understand better what we are attempting to "undo" in our students. Only by knowing what we are attempting to undo, can we better appreciate what our brand of education (and communication) is doing (see Berry, 1990).

In turn, we must reflect on what we, ourselves, are presuming as we teach, such as the beliefs and values we presume about speaking, listening, and learning. In time, we can then come to know better what at least some of our students are up against.

As with Mina and her teacher, so too for others can the paths of cultural reflection lead to mysterious places, including a critical distance from one's own familiar ways. By taking some time to walk and watch with each other, then, perhaps, we can design our actions—theories, practices, tools—with the intelligence of both in mind, knowingly creating our lives within the variety of available cultural views, helping each along our various ways. Proceeding in this way, giving each its proper due, suggests diagnosing our social ills, and designing elegant solutions for them, not by distributing some global critical manual for proper social and cultural and communicative conduct, but by carefully exploring the actual worlds of people and practices in particular places. So placed, situated in scenes of actual living, within cultural and communicative processes, we can then remain vigilantly watchful and cautious, so we do not—by championing our own way— mindlessly "eliminate" that which we failed to understand.

In the wake of the French Revolution, Vicomte de Chateaubriand expressed a similar thought when reflecting on what others considered to be the perhaps quaint or obsolete mysteries of their day: "There is nothing beautiful, pleasing, or grand in life, but that which is more or less mysterious. The most wonderful sentiments are those which produce impressions difficult to be explained ... It is a pitiful mode of reasoning to reject whatever we cannot comprehend." Perhaps Rising Wolf opens the door to a similar, underappreciated "beautiful, pleasing, or grand" mystery with his comments about "the communication between the animals and man," because communicating this Blackfeet way can "make you spiritually strong to the point that you just want to jump with cheer and joy." Failing to learn from these "difficult to be explained" thoughts, from the delightful cultural mysteries others' lives present for our own, would be pitiful indeed.

ACKNOWLEDGMENTS

I express deep thanks to the Blackfeet people, who gave me the gift of their time and words. Parts of this chapter were presented at the Ethnography of Communication Conference in Portland, Oregon, August 1992; at a forum on Discursive Psychology, Oxford, England, October, 1992; at the Applied Linguistics Conference on the Intercultural Communicator, Tampere, Finland, November, 1992; at the Institute for Psychology, Innsbruck, Austria, March, 1993; at the University of Massachusetts Conference on Ethnography and Qualitative Research in Education, June, 1994; and at many places since. An earlier version of this chapter appears as "I can't do that" but I can "actually see around corners," in J. Lehtonen (ed.), *Critical perspectives on communication research and pedagogy* (pp. 215–234), St. Ingbert, Germany:

Rohrig Universitatsverlag, 1995. That version of the essay has been re-printed in J. Martin, T. Nakayama, and L. Flores (Eds.), *Readings in cultural contexts* (pp. 160–172), Mountain View, CA: Mayfield, 1998.

ENDNOTES

1. The selection of a name for these people is not without some complica-tion. The people of concern here are members of the Blackfoot Confed-eracy, which consists of five tribes: the North Blackfoot, the Bloods, The North and the South Piegans, and the Small Robes, the latter being ex-terminated by smallpox and warfare. What were the South Piegans are now called, in English, the Blackfeet, referring to the only tribe of the Confederacy located in Montana, in the United States, with the others being in Canada. However, I am writing this version of history in Eng-lish, and it stands rather uneasily beside one inscribed in the Blackfoot or Siksika language. According to a Blackfoot: "In the Blackfeet lan-guage, the term Blackfeet is seldom, if ever, used to describe the Ameri-can tribe. The name Blackfeet is an exclusively English term. The Blackfoot language name of the tribe is Amskapi Pikuni, or South Peigans. Pikuni derives from an old form, meaning "Spotted Robes" (Darrell Robes Kipp, 1993, p.5). Because Robes Kipp goes on to use "Blackfeet" in his English writings, because this usage was adopted by my informants as well as my consultants, and because this is the typical way of referring to these people in English, I select this usage. The Blackfeet reservation in northern Montana consists of four different governmental districts: Browning, Heart Butte, Seville, and Old Agency. Most of my consultants and observations are centered in Browning, with a few from Heart Butte.

2. The cultural models of communication summarized here are based on earlier works with the Blackfeet (i.e., Carbaugh, 1993b, 1999, 2001). The larger project of which this chapter is a part involves additional studies, one exploring Blackfeet views of education, another a compara-tive analysis of Native American peoples' views of speaking, teaching, and learning, with a third exploring the implications of these views for a communication theory of language, culture, thought, and reality. Fol-lowing the Blackfeet, I use *Whiteman* and *White people* as cultural terms to characterize prominent people and their patterns in America today. Following Philips (1993, p. 16), I also use the term *Anglo* as a way of referring to traditions of communication that derive from an English heritage (see also Philips, 1993, p. 16). There is no ideal label for these patterns of practice, yet perhaps they are best identified as "prominent American" in that they are prominent in many scenes of America today, and are thus used by—or expected at times of—people in the United States from various heritages (racial, ethnic, or cultural). Exactly how such patterns play into these various scenes is an ongoing topic of my own research. See, for example, Carbaugh and Wolf (1999) for a discus-sion of Anglo–Native discourses in a court room.

3. Rising Wolf's poetic story is of course a verbal narration. What it narrates, however, or points to, is a kind of cultural communication that is not, itself, in its first instance, necessarily verbal (see chap. 7). In other words, the event he narrates is deeply communicative but is not itself a linguistic or verbal event. It is a spiritual and physical connection among things, beings. That it takes linguistic communication or a verbal narrative to describe that nonlinguistic event should not imply that the event being narrated, itself, is linguistic or verbal. This further underlines the importance of learning this kind of communication through watching, listening, and observing, through direct involvement in it, rather than through a secondary verbal discussion about it. This form of communication is the main theme of chapter 7.

4. The skill of speaking well, its association with elder males, and its use in disputes has deep historical roots in Blackfeet culture. One historian of the Blackfeet (Bryan, 1985) when writing about the Northern Plains Indians during the late 17th century noted as much: "Each band was led by a chief selected for his generosity, bravery and ability to speak well. Chiefs decided band movements and resolved internal disputes" (p. 56). See also Clements (2002).

5. Speaking in public however is just one activity within a whole cultural system of practice (Powell & Collier, 1990). That system, as a way of living, according to Beatrice Medicine (1994) derives from an equitable gender arrangement. She discusses American Indians prior to contacting the "Whiteman": "In most precontact societies, native women shared equally with men in social, economic, and ritual roles. Most ethnographic accounts (for the Plains culture area) emphasize the dynamic, dyadic interplay of both genders in the ongoing enterprise that allows indigenous societies to exist" (p. 67). She goes on to review some of the deleterious consequences to indigenous people of contacting the "Whiteman's" educational and legal systems. She concludes somewhat optimistically by noting that now, over one third of the "seven hundred American Indian and Alaska Native lawyers" educated since the 1970s are women. Whether and how these changes—adaptations to the "Whiteman's world"—pervade traditional Indian modes of communication, and the resulting conceptions and arrangements of gender roles in American Indian societies, needs investigation. For example, in 1985, Myrna Galbreath, became "one of the few Blackfeet women to be elected to a tribal leadership position" (Bryan, 1985, p. 71). Whether Blackfeet (and other peoples) deem this event to be culturally significant and if so, how so, needs further attention, especially focusing on the role of communication in executing such a position (e.g., as a woman in an elected position of tribal leadership).

A possible situation in which "speech anxiety" is reduced is a speech about oneself. A Blackfeet consultant explained that the "easiest speech to give is a speech about oneself." Presumably such a speech lays no claims to knowledge beyond oneself and is thus less featured in, but perhaps no less a part of the interconnected realm. The relation between Blackfeet models of person, self, verbal speaking, and the listener-active realm of "communicating with the animals and life around you," warrants much further attention. See Percy Bullchild (1985).

6. The importance and prominence of this elder speaking role is apparent in an advertisement for "The second annual Blackfeet Community College Traditional Encampment." Its first words are: "Join the elders and Blackfeet Community College for the second annual encampment. The elders will share knowledge and wisdom in the following areas: approaching an elder for assistance or knowledge ... story telling by elders and traditional people." From the "Official publication for the town of Browning and the Blackfeet Reservation," *Glacier Reporter*, July 6, 1989, p. 8.

⚜ 7 ⚜

"Just Listen": Blackfeet "Listening" and Landscape

What we need is a new definition [of landscape] ...
What chances does it offer for freedom of choice of
action? What chances for meaningful relationships with
other men and with the landscape itself? What chances for
individual fulfillment and for social change?

—John Brinckerhoff Jackson

Human beings have some talents, but not developed beyond those of
any one of the other forms of life. The special human ability is to com-
municate with other forms of life, learn from them all, and act as a fo-
cal point for things they wish to express. In any sacred location,
therefore, humans become the instrument by which all of creation is
able to interact and express its totality of satisfaction (1991, p. 38).

—Vine Deloria, Jr. (Sioux)

In native discourse, the local landscape falls neatly and repeatedly
into places—and places ... *are social constructions par excellence.*

—Keith Basso

How does one come to know places? What role does communication play in this process? In what follows, we find a very special kind of discursive and cultural resource at work. Specifically, in the following case, we explore a deeply significant form of "listening" used among some people known to themselves as *nizitapi* [real people], to others as Blackfeet, groups of men and women who have lived from the beginning in northern Montana, the United States.[1] When used in a special way by Blackfeet, the term, "listening," *refers* to a form of communication that is unique to them; when *enacted* in its special way, listening connects participants intimately to a specific physical and spiritual

100

place. Of main concern in what follows, then, is this cultural form of "listening" as it is being used by these people both as a cultural term about, and an enactment of communication. In this way, this form of communication refers to cultural practices in this particular community; in the conduct of these practices, Blackfeet people become linked intimately to physical spaces, thus providing for them a deep way of being and acting and dwelling in place.[2]

Recent discourse and culture studies have reminded us how intimately related cultural worlds and discursive practices indeed are (see Basso, 1990; Sherzer, 1987; Urban, 1991). At times in our daily routines, or as travelers, or as ethnographers, we can be quickly reminded of this, especially when we lose our place in the world. In a moment, we may become perplexed as to where we are, with the perplexity deepening if our available discourse is less than nuanced about that place. What we should do, next, may confound us, for willful and efficacious action can hinge completely on proper assessments of the place we are in. Without knowing the place, we are unsure how to act. Discourses of place thus suggest cultural actions, yet any one place might suggest multiple cultural discourses. We may think we know something, through a discourse, yet this knowing may be somewhat out of its cultural place, as when one ascends a small hill for lunch, only to find later that one's lunch site was a sacred burial mound. In retrospect, we find our habitual action and cultural knowledge were somehow out of place. Caught in moments like these—a place without a discourse, or a discourse out of its place— we can feel displaced, or dislocated. Cultural places without their discourses, or discourses out of their cultural place, each shows only part of a picture, an underexposed view, suggesting how each can work with the other to form a more vivid joint production.

Early on, Benjamin Lee Whorf (1941/1956) explored ways situated, "habitual thought and behavior" was related to, and could be used to deepen our understandings of routine linguistic patterns, exploring mainly how cultural action related to, what he called, "fashions of speaking." How is it that people, and different peoples, act in the world; how does that habitual action, and differences in action, relate to their patterns of language use? A legacy of Whorf, and Edward Sapir, has been the suggested linking of cultural patterns of behavior and thought with linguistic routines. One ethnographic way of studying discourse and culture has been so developed, thus, to explore peoples' linguistic patterns as cultural routines (e.g., Hymes 1981). A small and recent group of ethnographic work has explored how fashions of speaking relate to places. Studies by Gerry Philipsen (1976) and Keith Basso (1996) have drawn attention to ways discourse keeps the past and places, that is, cultural traditions, alive in

the present.[3] Related works have been reexamining "linguistic relativity," especially how languages relate people differently to various cultural situations and the "natural" thoughts active in them (see, e.g.,
Gumperz & Levinson, 1996; Lucy, 1992; Samuels, 2001). All remind
us how deeply discourse and language are being variously fashioned
by people in, and about place.

Place itself, therefore, can enter rather dramatically as a special
kind of contextual concern in cultural and communication studies (see
Feld & Basso, 1996). At least for some people, places can (and do)
"speak," if only we—citizens and scholars alike—take the time to "listen" accordingly. Auditing communication processes in this way can
help all of us learn more about places, about ourselves, about others,
about how "we" are related, about what we can (and should) do, about
how we can (and should) feel. There is, I think, much we can learn
from listening to places through discourses and cultures. The results
can be surprising, even mysterious. We may find, as a way of knowing
places, a linguistic cultural routine, or at other times, a nonlinguistic
means. Whether the latter involves cultural communication outside of
language, I cannot say, at least not here, through this printed medium.
The irony of discussing in words a way of knowing places that is, I believe, in a cultural sense, at least partially nonlinguistic, should not escape our notice. For some places can teach us much more than we can
willfully and verbally communicate. Learnings can radiate, then, from
places, into various discursive ways, including the verbal and nonverbal ways of knowing [them]. Places, in other words, can communicate
beyond words, if only we listen.

Yet of course, when writing of these matters, we use words. And my
effort here occurs in a place of its own. Thus, what I put forth here is a
kind of "translation" of one form of a Blackfeet cultural discourse—"listening" among Blackfeet—into another—writing among
academics. This occurs through one channel and genre of "presentation," a written essay or chapter. As such, the presentation is designed, for the most part but not exclusively, for a nonnative
population, although several Native readers and listeners have read
or heard, encouraged and commented on it. My general hope is that
all readers are invited to revisit the intimate relations between linguistic and nonlinguistic discourses, and ways these are linked to
cultures and places. What I seek to offer is an ethnographic narrative
about such concerns, organized more specifically to suggest the following: that discourse and culture come hand in hand; that senses of
place run deeply into cultural discourses; that these can include communication forms that may be, in large part, nonlinguistic; and further that some cultural uses of discourse and language, such as the
directive to "just listen," can, for some people, presume this basic,

nonlinguistic communication process, as a kind of cultural action prior to language. We shall bear in mind, then, in what follows, both the link between linguistic discourse and place, and the non-linguistic meditative acts such places can invite and create. In fact we must do so, if we are to honor the cultural place of this discourse. If we do not, we risk, again, dislocating those people from the places to which they listen, in which they dwell.[4]

A DISCURSIVE PRACTICE AND CULTURAL PLACES

Two Bears had left a message for me with the front desk personnel of the Museum of the Plains Indian.[5] His windshield had been smashed by vandals the night before. He would have to make a trip some 45 miles east to Cut Bank to get a new one. "Please be patient," the museum personnel told me. "He'll be back shortly after nine o'clock." Having been through the museum several times over the years, and repeatedly this summer, I took the opportunity to walk outside and enjoy the warm July breeze. I considered walking the couple of blocks back to my family's apartment, but decided to relax in the sun, watch the wind roll over the plains, and enjoy the view of the Rocky Mountain Range to the west—the "backbone of the world," as the Blackfeet have called it.

While doing so, my mind wondered to the apparent contrasts in front of me on that morning, a museum of traditional artifacts amid a diverse and complex set of contemporary lives, a town site of 80% unemployment amid a pristine, powerful landscape, and a vandalized windshield for a cultural spokesperson of the Blackfeet Nation.

As I was soaking in the morning sun and these thoughts, I noticed a van pull up. Sure enough, at around 9:30 a.m., Two Bears had arrived. He had agreed the day before to show me and three others around the reservation, and so he motioned for us to come, indicating that he was ready to go. As we crawled into his van, he talked about the "kids who prowl Browning's main street at night" and for some reason target windshields with their rocks. "It cost about $300 to replace it," he said.

As we drove down Browning's Main Street, Two Bears told us: "There are about 15,000 enrolled Blackfeet tribal members. About 7,000 live on the reservation." Of these, "about four to five percent practice traditional Blackfeet ways." Earlier—in 1979–1980, in 1985, and in 1989—I had talked with several tribal members who were living the traditional Blackfeet ways, navigating "the modern-day world" through their own traditional practices. Two Bears, Rising Wolf, Slow Talker, and others had explained to me that these provided a rich pool of social resources for contemporary living. Driving down the Main

Street of Browning, however, it was difficult for me to envision these cultural ways being practiced here.

On the eastern outskirts of town, Two Bears swerved across the road, drove into a pull-off, and without any warning, continued right out into a field. Almost knocked off my seat, I realized we were following some invisible dirt path which eventually emptied right onto the plains. Rumbling along, I noticed we were situated in a bit of a small bowl, with one very slight ridge around the bowl being created a century earlier by the tracks of the Great Northern Railway.

As I pondered the railway, Two Bears informed us that we were nestled into a site of traditional activities. "This," Two Bears told us, "is a sacred site, the site of the Sun Dance." As we looked around, I noticed the remains of five Sun Lodges. The custom is that each was to be used only once. Asking us not to take any pictures—"The elders request that this site be treated as sacred with no pictures taken"—Two Bears recounted the Blackfeet tale of Scar Face, of a young disfigured boy who was healed by the Sun and thus was able to gather the favor of a pretty young woman. We stood in silence awhile.

Two Bears asked:

> Did you ever pray to the sun or leave an offering for the sun? It is the source of light, warmth, and makes things grow. We believe we should be thankful for that ... Our religion tells us that all of this (waving his arm broadly) is connected. The rocks, the grass, the sun. The pipes that we use in our ceremonies are made of stone (he shapes his hands as a bowl). The stone represents the earth (his hands become a globe). The stem is made of wood. It represents all living things. The smoke of the pipe is like a spirit. You see it briefly, then it disappears, up to the Creator. We believe that all things are connected like this.

Two Bears invites us into a prolonged period of silence, to pray, meditate, or leave an offering—"usually of tobacco"—if we wished. Each of us quietly move away by ourselves to look at the lodges and pray. After a long, silent, reflective period at this sacred site, we slowly gather to leave. As we move to the van, finding it hard to leave the site, Two Bears pauses, looks around him at the grass, at the lodges, at the small rolling ridges immediately surrounding us, at the grand mountains in the distance, at the beautiful blue sky. Feeling the warmth of the sun, the coolness of the breeze, and hearing the meadowlarks warble, he is visibly delighted: "If you have a problem, or can't find an answer for something, our belief is that you can come out here, or to the mountains, or just about anywhere, sit down and listen. If you sit and listen patiently, you'll find an answer."

We stood together silently for a few more moments, then quietly crawled into the van.

As we drove across the vast plains, Two Bears developed the idea of "sitting and listening" by describing "fasting" and other activities associated with traditional ceremonies. This prompted him to comment further about how some Indians market sacred ceremonies for the public, here in the United States and in Europe. "That's crooked. It's just wrong to put a price on religious things," he said.

Moving further out onto the open plains, we turned down a bumpy road coming to a stop on a slight rise, able to see the vast open prairie and the beauty of the plains. Two Bears turned to us and suggested something, his way of being in such a place:

> You can come out here and sit down. Just sit down and listen. In time, you might hear a raven and realize that raven is saying something to you. Or you might talk to a tree. But you have to listen. Be quiet. Be patient. The answer will come to you ... We are realists. We are part of all of this (gesturing to the plains, to the immense "backbone" of mountains to the west, trees, grass). We listen to this.

After a couple of hours and many miles of driving through several parts of the reservation's lands, we wound our way deep into an inner sanctuary, to what we learn from Two Bears is a geographic site rich with potential for contemporary living and deep with the lessons of history. Down a long dirt road, over a bridge, up on a small ridge, through two fences, again, we are no longer on a visible road, just driving across prairie grass. We stop, look over several small ridges, notice some distant cliffs of multicolored rock. Just over a close rise, a beautiful verdant valley reveals itself, a hidden emerald scene amidst a sea of golden grasses. Two Bears's thoughts turn to his contemporaries: "This would be an ideal place for those of our people having trouble with drugs or alcohol. They could come out here and think about things. It's ideal for that."

As we stand on top of a small ridge, we overlook a meandering stream punctuated with large Cottonwood trees, banks thickly covered with reeds and grasses, an oasis amid a golden brown prairie. His thoughts bring the past to the present. He explains how his ancestors ran buffalo across these ridges, guiding them through a kind of grandly orchestrated "V" of flags and stones to jump off the cliff right here. The scale of the event, covering miles, was huge and impressive. As we walk to the base of the cliff, I am amazed at the quantity of buffalo bones and teeth evident, all of which create a deep, several inch layer in the earth's surface. Signs of an immediate past lay right here. We find stones, "scrapers," used to rub buffalo flesh from hide. Twice Two Bears motions to the cliff above and the valley floor below:

> Imagine from down below here, buffalo coming over the cliff, men tending to them, drinking buffalo blood, eating the marrow, roasting and eat-

ing the back meat, women cutting the other meat into strips and drying it in the sun. Kids excited and running around. Imagine how exciting of a time it was. Everyone was happy.

As we walk from the small valley up the hill to leave, Two Bears stops and reflects:

Just listen

> (a pause of about 1 minute reveals utter tranquility, a few birds sing, followed by a magnificent silence and stillness with no distant sound—of cars, planes, trains—to be heard)

Once I heard a mountain lion down there (gesturing to the stream).

Have you ever heard one? You'll never forget it.

This is an ideal place to come.

While riding back to the Museum, a German woman asks Two Bears how he learned all that he knew. "I was raised by my grandmother who knew the traditional ways. Every night she would tell me a story." Then laughing he adds, "And if she didn't think I was listening, I'd be told the same story the next night!" We all laugh. Two Bears then tells us a few traditional Blackfeet stories about the complex trickster, Napi. Eventually, we arrive at the Museum, each giving Two Bears "payment" for the day, what he calls an "offering."

Starting with a shattered windshield, and now well into the beautifully sunset evening, Two Bears was exhausted. He asks me to call him in the morning. We'd have to get together again, he says, perhaps at his encampment, stay in his lodge, have some Swiss steak, visit some people there.

As was typical after spending time with him, I was saturated and content as I made my way back to my apartment.

"LISTENING" AS A FORM OF CULTURAL COMMUNICATION: A COMPLEX MESSAGE ABOUT COMMUNICATION ITSELF

How is it, as Two Bears says above, when one has "a problem" or "can't find an answer," one can go to a special place, "sit down and listen"? How can it be, if you do this, "you'll find an answer"? Or how is it that "you might hear a raven," or "talk to a tree," or listen "to a mountain lion"? Or, if you are "quiet" and "patient," "the answer will come to you"? Why is it that a remote, verdant valley is "an ideal place" for "our people having trouble with drugs or alcohol"? And how is it that this "place" is a good one in which "to think about things"? Is this largely a metaphor as a way of saying something? Or is there a Blackfeet culture in which this form of living and these expressive practices are quite real? If so, what cultural features are active in these communicative practices? In short, what Blackfeet premises make these practices make sense?

In this day's activities and commentary by Two Bears, there appears repeatedly a prominent symbolic category, *and* a prominent form of symbolic practice, *listening*. A site of Sun Lodges, a vast prairie, a verdant valley, each demonstrates a scene in which the term, *listening*, and the practice of listening, are being used by Two Bears both to describe his life in its cultural place, and to enact a traditional way of dwelling there. Communicating through this and related terms, and conducting this and related practices provides for Two Bears and other Blackfeet people, a significant and forceful cultural form of action.

In the moments of social interaction described, Two Bears uses language that is intimately linked to and motivated by the immediate physical and cultural landscape in which he finds himself. For example, Two Bears informs us of a shared belief, "our belief that you can come out here, or to the mountains, or just about anywhere, sit down and listen." The immediate landscape is thus composed of a combination of physical and cultural qualities. Within this place, so conceived, Two Bears says, is created a cultural motive for listening. The place thus invites a cultural form of action, listening, with that form of action being attentive to the site as something to which it is worth our while to listen. His plea to us to listen, then, is aroused by the place, just as the place becomes full of significance through this cultural form. In this practice of listening, an activity and place become intimately entwined, for this cultural form and this natural site reveal themselves together.

This cultural practice by Two Bears, here, is a complex communication process. Part of the complexity involves the way a verbal message is being used to draw attention to a prominent nonverbal means of communicating. For example, in his oral utterance to us about listening, in this landscape, he is commenting about a nonoral act of listening to this landscape. This nonverbal act is itself a deeply cultural form of action in which the Blackfeet persona and the physical place become intimately linked, in a particularly Blackfeet way. To listen this way—that is, in the way Two Bears mentions, and does, here—is thus to be linked to a place and to be linked to a place this way is to live within it, at least partly, through this nonverbal form of listening. Further, Two Bears's comment, itself, "that you can come out here ... sit down and listen," follows directly from his very nonverbal act of listening in this place. The Blackfeet person and place thus become inseparably linked. As Two Bears' actions demonstrate here: One should listen to places; then one can sensibly make a linguistic reference to this listening form; with this form, in the first instance, being a nonlinguistic mode of learning from, and inhabiting places.[6]

Some kinds of places are apparently more appropriate for this kind of Blackfeet "listening" than are others, although—according to Two Bears—"just about anywhere" might do. Examples of such places that Two Bears mentions are "here" or "out here" on the quiet plains, "this" verdant valley, the former buffalo jump as "an ideal place," or "the mountains," each being a place where "sitting and listening" can (and should) be done.

Elsewhere, and many years earlier (in 1980), while first hiking in a stunning, beautiful, and remote valley along the Rocky Mountain front, assuming I was alone, I stumbled upon a Blackfeet man sitting by himself, colored cloth tied to a tree close to him. At the time I was a bit dumbstruck by the site. I understand his action, now, on reflection, to be a "listening" one. During other similar events such as spiritual encampments, when on a prominent ridge, in a glade of trees, or on an open meadow, one might find others in such a scene. In such places, one can on occasion see others, or engage oneself in acts of listening. Two Bears says "just about anywhere" might do,[7] but there are particularly "ideal" places for listening. But why these places?

Each of these and similar places carry qualities that are conducive to certain kinds of cultural practices. The best apparently combine three, a visual scene of natural beauty, an aural tone of tranquility, and a history of valued cultural activity. For example, the Sun Lodges sit in a pleasant natural bowl, far enough from a state highway to be accessible yet generally quiet, and a known historical site of a most sacred ceremony, the Sun Dance. The buffalo jump memorializes historical activities, in a splendidly tranquil place, bountiful with nature's beauty. Ideal places for listening combine these three qualities together, a weaving of naturalistic beauty, solemnity, and historical tradition, thus transforming nature's sites into culture's sacred scenes, places that invite, can speak, and in turn be re-created through the listening form.

The link between sacredness, place, and the listening form can be a strong one. For example, those familiar with the salient cultural heritage can attend nonverbally to the remains of the Sun Lodges, and begin seeing and hearing the sacred activities, the excitement, the ways of living that have occurred there for years. The past, and all it represents, comes alive through listening in this present place. Similarly, at the buffalo jump, listening brings to the fore the life this place has sustained, and all that it now physically embodies. In these historical, tranquil, and beautiful places, the land speaks. What it says, and what one can hear, is sacred. Through the process, listening keeps tradition alive in the present, remaking it in current circumstances, and thus remembering—or identifying with—landscapes as sacred places; all of this, from a physical site to the reconstruction of a traditional cultural scene, comes to life through the listening form.

There is another, important cultural sense in which sacredness, place, and listening are interrelated. Here, however, it is not so much that a place is already heard and known as a sacred place, as it is assumed that almost any place—"just about anywhere," according to Two Bears—might reveal sacredness to a listener. In a city watching a small child, marveling at the intricate patterns in a stone, watching a spider in the corner of the living room, all might suggest sacredness to a listener. Situated activities as these might suggest something spiritual to a listener. And one should be open to this ever-present feature in the world. "Listening," then, can be doubly placed as a cultural attentiveness to a known sacred place, and to the sacredness in just about any place. As a way of dwelling, the cultural form thus attunes to, and contributes to the creation of the sacred.

Are there specific acts that comprise listening as a cultural form of action? Two Bears mentioned several: "You can come out here ... sit down and listen ... sit and listen patiently"; "You have to listen. Be quiet. Be patient"; you can "think"; "You might hear." Listening this way can involve the listener in an intense, efficacious, and complex set of communicative acts in which one is not speaking, discussing, or disclosing, but sitting quietly, watching, and feeling the place, through all the senses. Presumed for the acts is an active co-presence with the natural and historical place in which, and to which one listens. The belief is that one can—at some times more than others—eventually "hear" and learn from it. Such acts are thus not so much internally focused on one's meditative self, but externally focused on one's place through an active attentiveness to that scene, to the highly active powers and insights it offers. In the process, one becomes a part of the scene, hearing and feeling with it.

When involved in such action, from a Blackfeet view, to what might one listen; or, what might one hear? There are many potential instruments and sources of messages being made available through this cultural form. Two Bears brings several to his commentary: "You might hear a raven and realize that raven is saying something to you"; "You might talk to a tree"; "I heard a mountain lion"; or, in short, as "realists," "We listen to [all of] this." The raven, the tree, the mountain lion, all of the animals, plants, rocks, water, trees, breeze, and so on can "speak," if one just listens. Each thus can be consulted and listened to as a source of important, inspirational, and powerful messages. The belief that the natural world is expressively active is, according to Two Bears, not a fanciful nor farcical mysticism, but a Blackfeet kind of realism. People, animals, rocks, and trees are *actually* co-present and co-participant with people as embodiments of the spirit(s) in the world. Attending to this "real" world is a key motive for listening, and renders animals and trees and places generally as spirited speakers to—and thus as potentially hearable by—us all. This is something widely accessible, if only we listen appropriately.[8]

As a consequence of this belief, Blackfeet who use this form have access to powerful messages, and can share the potential benefits of attending to "all of this," as Two Bears says. As Vine Deloria (1991) put it in our opening quote, humans have the "special ability" to learn "to communicate with other forms of life." (p. 38). And further, "the myriad forms of life which inhabit the land require specific forms of communication and interaction" (p. 38). One such form is listening, with its attentiveness to cultural and physical places, to actions and specific sites, to tradition, the natural and present world.

Yet, how does one know what a place "says"? The knowledge does not necessarily come easily. And much hinges on the listener. In fact, particular revelations may, but need not necessarily take days or years. Whatever the time frame, the objective of meditating on who and where we are, what it all means, and the means for doing so—through an active silence in place—remains the same. One listens to that immediately real, historically transmitted, spiritually infused, deeply interconnected world, to that complex arrangement in order better to understand that of which one is inevitably a small part.

The communicative process, so conceived and acted in a Blackfeet way, can also expose one as an "other" who, for whatever reasons, is somewhat deaf to these messages, doesn't quite hear them, and was caught not listening.

I was walking with Two Bears up a small trail from the valley floor to the cliff above. I was reflecting upon the hunting skills of the earlier Blackfeet community, the vibrant traditional encampments, practices that connected generations of people to each other and their places through these cultural activities. We walked slowly, quietly, sun on our backs, a refreshing breeze on our faces. Occasionally in the earth I would see a buffalo tooth, jaw, or other bone. I could hear the rustling of the wind through the short prairie grass that is unique on these northern plains. The water moved along the stream bed, adding a trickling sound to the rustling of the grass. Captured by my thoughts, I was reveling in the tranquility and solitude of the place. Two Bears turned to me and asked: "Did you get that?" My first thought was, "Get what?" I didn't hear anything. Immersed in my own reflections, I had missed something. Prompted by Two Bears's question, somehow I was able to call up from my mind's recesses an earlier and distant raven's call, "caw caw caw." Two Bears's wry smile brought to mind the immediate point of his question. Well, yes, I thought, I guess I did hear something. But the distant bird I heard was, to Two Bears, saying something worthy of comment. The raven had spoken. I wondered out loud, "What did the raven say?" Two Bears responded: "He's talkin' to ya."

But what did he say, I wondered? Before I asked, I realized I had already asked this kind of question before on other occasions, several—if not too many—times. The answer was always the same. "This is for the listener to decide. The meaning will be the listener's."[9]

I was delighted at how seamlessly listening had worked its way into Two Bears's routines, but also reminded once again of my own habitual ways, focused as they often are to hear the human over the animal, the individual person above the activities of the place, the linguistic thought over the audible nonverbal, and to Blackfeet, deeply communicative activities. Yes, indeed, Two Bears had reminded me to listen, and this meaning was mine.

The kind of listening invoked here by Two Bears functions in a complex way: it is a carrier of cultural content, a historical way of being that invokes that history in the present; one recalls for example the encampment at the buffalo jump, one's ancestors and the values in traditional lives and ways; it is also a means of connecting with places, like these, and all that makes them what they are, rocks, ravens and trees included; it is further a deeply historical kind of conduct itself. As such, listening provides a traditional way of actively co-participating in a largely nonoral, nonverbal, yet real and spiritual world. Through this traditional kind of listening, one can become part of a multidimensional realm of nonspoken activity that is emphatically real, highly communicative, inspiring, personally rewarding, and deeply meditative.

In its proper physical and cultural place, this communicative act is adamantly actual and can involve deeply significant consultations with nonhuman spirits and powers that are active in the world. Note that Two Bears emphasizes—and repeatedly in our discussions—what he calls a "realism," a declaration of a cultural reality that integrates objects and people and spirits into a world that can be and should be "heard." The process of connecting with and learning from this world is especially pronounced and amplified in traditional ceremonies of fasting or in vision quests (e.g., Ewers, 1958, pp. 162 ff.; McClintock, 1992, pp. 354–367; Schultz & Donaldson, 1930, esp. pp. 48–69). One's hope in these acts is based on one's faith that this process will open a spiritual and natural world for one's inspection and thus allow one protection from harm, a renewal of power, and a deeper understanding of one's place within the real forces at work in a complex and at times unfriendly world.

The form is of particular, practical importance as a general way of being and dwelling in place. For example, Two Bears heard the raven say something to him, in this deeply historical site, with the raven's communication offering something worthy of comment. During troubled times, the form can reveal insights through special places where some help may appear. For example, Two Bears mentions how "a problem" one has, or lack of "an answer" one seeks, may invite certain insights from a proper listening place. When listening, there, to its powerful messages, one should not expect, but one might "find an answer." Similarly, when seeking, or when one has "trouble with alcohol or drugs," one can silently listen in a proper place. Through the form, one might gain greater protection from harm and deepen one's understanding. The form offers a way of being that is ever open to the insights places can suggest. The form, thus, can open a sensed imperfection to nonverbal, real, sensible features—the active agents—in the world, some of which can act in quite surprising ways, thereby offering corrective insights, an enhanced sense of power and place within that world.

There is the potential for mystery in this listening process that is important to emphasize.[10] One does not make listening happen through an assertion of one's own will. In fact, efforts to listen this way will likely fail. In other words, one can put oneself in a proper place to listen, but the success and quality of the process is something that issues forth from the place, coming along of its own. On special occasions, and if good fortune permits, the spirits in the world can come in ways that defy normal expectations, and reveal sacred truths. The hope and faith associated with the action is captured when Two Bears claims: "sit and listen patiently, you'll find an answer," or "The answer will come to you." But again, listening is not a product one makes and wills for oneself; it is a gift from that world in which one lives, coming sometimes, as Percy Bullchild (1985) says, through "the power of mystery." In this sense, within this Blackfeet form, one can be opened to uncontrollable, real, powerful, sacred forces in the world and should open one's self to knowing and understanding them. These can and will fashion what one hears, feels, and will become. A proper affective attitude, in these moments, is humility within what is potentially a quite potent and sacred scene, asking pity for one's feeble self, seeking sympathy and compassion because one has been placed in the presence of possibly uncontrollable and overwhelming forces. In the process, the spirits of the cultural and physical scene become figured largely over and through oneself, the actor. The belief is, if not immediately then eventually, the form in place, sometimes infused with the power of mystery, will yield potent and powerful insights that are of deep and enduring value (e.g., insights into life's perplexing nature and enhanced power as an actor).[11]

To refer to listening, then, as Two Bears does, or to enact it, is to invoke a complex cultural communicative form; it is a form that derives from and helps constitute cultural and physical places; it provides a traditional, nonverbal way of being in those places; it invites various entities as spirited co-participants in this communication; it valorizes and intensely activates the nonoral communicative acts of watching, listening, and sensing nonverbally; it offers a deeply historical way of consulting the traditions and current cosmic arrangement of places as an aid to the various contingencies of contemporary life. Blackfeet listening is thus a highly reflective and revelatory mode of communication that can open one to the mysteries of unity between the physical and the spiritual, to relationships between natural and human forms, and to links between places and persons, all the while providing protection, power, and enhanced knowledge of one's small place in the world.

ACTIVE PLACES AND PEOPLE:
A BLACKFEET CULTURAL DISCOURSE

An interpretation of the aforementioned cultural communicative form can be summarized through a series of cultural propositions. This brings into sharper view a system of traditional Blackfeet beliefs and morals about dwelling (living in place), doing (proper action), feeling (emotion expression), and being (identity).[12] The system is offered here simply as a kind of summary of relevant premises as they are active in the listening form. Clearly, there are other, related premises for other forms of action. The following relevant and incomplete set of propositions offer my interpretation of Blackfeet beliefs and morals in "listening."

To listen in this Blackfeet way is to "dwell in the world" based upon basic realist beliefs about, and a moral for acting within that world. The basic beliefs are these: Things, people, animals, and places are interconnected in ways that are knowable, and unknowable; spirits exist in things, people, animals, and places. The basic moral imperative: People should be attentive and attuned to this.

As a form of communication conduct, listening is a practice, or "way of doing" something. Basic beliefs about this action are these: People's actions are part of this interconnected world; people can and should listen to this world; by listening, people can become attuned to this world; becoming attuned to this is good.

Listening also suggests a "range of feeling" and various objects of feeling. Basic beliefs about emotion are: People can feel (and see) the interconnectedness of things, places, and people; when tuned into this, feeling is integrated through things, places, and people: This is good; when not tuned into this, people feel confused, sad, and down.

Finally, and in summary, listening is a "way of being" that involves these basic beliefs about identity: Traditional Blackfeet acts are intimately situated in cultural, especially reservation places; the reservation is a place, and traditional places where people can actively live, and are motivated by those places to live in the proper way; this way re-creates the basic beliefs about dwelling, doing, and feeling that are activated in, and by, those very places.

These cultural propositions concerning listening-as-a-way-of-dwelling-in-place, when socially active, situate people in place, create particular cultural places, and spiritually animate those places with actors that are human and nonhuman. Dwelling in such places among such actors is to be living in a special physical culturescape or scene. To be there is not just a belief about this place, but a moral imperative that one dwell in such a place, at least at times, in this proper and particular way.

The basic belief about acting mentioned here, again, focuses our attention on listening. As elaborated, this form of action is a morally sanctioned way of becoming attuned to, and learning from, a complex spiritual and natural world. Basic beliefs about emotion are activated through this cultural process as animals, trees, and places generally become objects of positive and sometimes intense emotion. One learns that such things are real, alive, and worthy of respect and deep feeling. Realizing this can, as Rising Wolf put it to me, "make you jump with cheer and joy."

These basic propositions, when active, as in the traditional listening form, constitute both conditions for and enactments of a Blackfeet discourse, a way of being a person that is intimately situated in places, dwelling a particular way while there, cultivating proper feelings about the place, its features and people, such that this way of being and these places become inextricably intertwined.

"LISTENING" IN OTHER CULTURAL SCENES

The Pawnee and Otoe American Indian writer, Anna Lee Walters, has recently published a series of autobiographical stories. In a telling and early passage she writes:

> Listening is the first sense to develop in the womb. It is not surprising, then, that I was conscious of sounds earlier than anything else as an infant. Mainly, these were the sounds of the universe, the outdoors. They included whishing bird wings rising up into the sky, rustling trees, the cry of the mourning dove, and the rippling wind (Walters, 1992, p. 12).

In one of Walters' stories, she describes a dialogue between an old man and a visitor. The wise old sage sat at night watching the visitor for over an hour. He then formulated a lesson and its moral for his visitor in these words:

> It is important and curious to remember that everything we two-leggeds know about being human, we learned from the four-leggeds, the animals and birds, and everything else in the universe. None of this knowledge is

solely your own ... All these creatures and beings out here talk ... Even today. They told our elders a lot ...

Listen ...

Old folks always say that the distance between two-leggeds and
four-leggeds nowadays hasn't changed four-leggeds in any way. The distance has only changed us two-leggeds, made us worse off, more pitiful.
They say the four-leggeds still talk the way they always have. It's we
who've forgotten to listen. (Walters, 1992, pp. 30–32)

As Walters creates her stories here, one autobiographical, the other
a morality tale, she uses a cultural form. Just as the old sage implores
his visitor to listen, so she implores her reader to step into that form of
communication, into that way of dwelling in place and feeling about it.
Through this form, she instructs us how important lessons can be
learned, problems in one's life can be addressed, inspiration gained,
with our personal capacities for understanding and living in the world
being richly enhanced in the process. Hopefully, by now, as a result of
the analyses just given, the depth and potential of this form has become more discernible, as a way of linking people to their places, its
landscapes and all that that includes.

A failure to understand such a form can lead outsiders to quick and
disastrous judgments. An author of a recent book on Native American
Indian issues reported a discussion between himself and a Warm
Springs Indian concerning land use and management. The Indian had
told him: "Listen to the things that [have] no mouths" (Bordewich, 1996,
p. 157). Later, while discussing the controversial placement of a large
astronomical observatory on top of Mount Graham in Arizona, a mountain deemed sacred to some Apache people, he ran into a similar admo-
nition. Bordewich was told, in the Apache Indian's words, that "silence
was a form of piety." In so many gestures, the Indians were saying something like this: "We know what we know, deeply, by listening in this
place. This is all we can report to you. To say more is to discredit and
dishonor our way of knowing and being in our sacred places." The ad-
monition aroused a bewildered disbelief in the outsider who formulated
his reply in this way: Representatives of the Indians "were presenting silence as the ultimate argument ... To say nothing was to say everything
... It was a stunning argument. In lieu of fact, they offered mystery and a
blank slate" (Bordewich, 1996, p. 218). To the outsider, such actions
were nearly incomprehensible, and clearly unsatisfactory.

Needless to say, he did not have available to him an understanding
nor appreciation of listening to such places, and hearing what they had
to say. Neither, apparently, did he understand how that form itself is a
deeply historical root of identity that others can easily uproot, quickly
cast aside, and leave to wither in the heat of their own day.

This is the kind of reaction one can anticipate when two largely incommensurate, culturally based practices, run into one another. For the one valorizes listening as a communicative form, activates shared beliefs about what that makes available, and utilizes silence as a communal means for increasing understanding of oneself and one's environment; for the other, speaking is valorized as a communicative form, with beliefs being constructed upon deliberative "facts," and verbal activity providing the primary means for knowing oneself and one's places. To each, the other is not quite right. And thus, the relations between each can strain the identities at work in such places, setting a scene for contesting people and places, too often nurturing only one at the expense of another (see Carbaugh & Wolf, 1999).

And so it goes, as culturally based forms give birth to different cultural realities, different linguistic and communicative practices, different senses of dwelling in places, of acting and feeling there, of identity and location. By attending to the role of discursive practices in individual and cultural lives, especially those connecting people to place, perhaps we can create a better understanding of communication, especially of each about the other. Perhaps further, we can increase the expressive means available to each of us for our own understandings, and for deeper insights, from personal to global ecologies, if we just listen accordingly.

ACKNOWLEDGMENTS

Portions of this research were presented at the Conference on Narrative and Identity, Institute for Cultural Studies, Vienna, Austria, December 1995; as the Keynote Address at the Conference on Narrative Psychology and Place, University of Turin, Italy October 1996; at the National Communication Association, San Diego, California, November 1996; and as the Keynote Address of the Southwest Communication Association, Arizona State University-West, April, 1997. My thanks to Jens Brockmeier, Carla Barbisio, Young Kim, Charles Braithwaite, and Dawn Braithwaite, respectively, for arranging these opportunities and to the participants for their lively discussions. Special thanks to Betsy Bach of the University of Montana for making an extended stay in Montana possible during the summer of 1989. Portions of this research were funded by a grant from the Office of Research Affairs, University of Massachusetts. My deepest thanks to many Blackfeet who have offered their time and knowledge and places. I have tried to listen carefully and, as always, the meaning here is the listener's. An earlier version of this essay appears as Carbaugh (1999).

ENDNOTES

1. Several Blackfeet authors have produced writings about Blackfeet culture and history, including oral histories (e.g., Bullchild, 1985; Hungry Wolf, 1980; Long Lance, 1928), overviews of Blackfeet life (Kipp, 1993; Long Standing Bear Chief, 1992), thematic inscriptions of Blackfeet heritage (e.g., Ground, 1978; Rides at the Door, 1979) and a superb set of novels (e.g., Welch, 1974, 1987a, 1987b). Traditional ethnographic studies by others about Blackfeet culture are also available (e.g., Bradley, 1923; Goldfrank, 1945; Lewis, 1941, 1942; McClintock, 1992; Wissler, 1911, 1918; Wissler & Duvall, 1908) as is a comprehensive dictionary of the Blackfoot language (Frantz & Russell, 1995). A popular series of essays appeared early in this century written by James Willard Schultz, who married a Blackfeet woman (1907/1983, 1962, 1988; also see Grinnell, 1962, and Schultz & Donaldson, 1930). More recent examinations are those by Dempsey (1972, 1994), Ewers (1958), Kidd (1986), and McFee (1968, 1977). None of these studies sustain a focus on communication itself, social interaction, and contemporary cultural life. Others have studied communication among other Native American peoples (e.g., Basso, 1996; Braithwaite, 1997; Darnell, 1988; Foley, 1995; Hymes, 1981; Philips, 1993; R. Scollon & S. Scollon, 1981; Weider & Pratt, 1990, 1993). For recent discussions of American Indian identity and cultural domination see Medicine (1994) and O'Neill (1994), among others.

2. The following analyses employ a basic ethnographic orientation discussed in detail elsewhere (Carbaugh & Hastings, 1992; Hymes, 1972; Philipsen, 1989). The specific communicative activity of concern in this chapter is both a cultural term for *communicative action* (i.e., listening) and the activities so designated. The analysis is conducted by using a conceptual heuristic designed especially for such culturally based, metapragmatic terms, and practices, like this listening form (Carbaugh, 1989). This conceptual system has been productively used in various qualitative and quantitative studies (e.g., Baxter, 1993; Baxter & Goldsmith, 1990; Bloch, 2003; Garrett, 1993; Hall & Valde, 1995; Scollo Sawyer, 2004).

   The particular findings reported here derive from a corpus of data collected periodically over the past years (during parts of 1979, 1980, 1985, 1989, 1996, 1997, 2002, 2004) amounting to about 2 years of fieldwork. The specific analytical procedure can be summarized as following these general phases: (1) a discovery and observation in two parts, (a) of a focal term or phrase about communicative action that is prominent, potent, and recurrent in a cultural scene or community, as well as (b) the symbolic enactments the term makes relevant; (2) a detailed description, respectively, of both (a) the actual, routine linguistic practices that make use of the specific term, and (b) enactments of the focal communicative action as it is done in everyday scenes; (3) an analysis of these discursive enactments as culturally situated acts in events, exploring how each employs the distinctive form of communicative action; and (4) an interpretation of the communal meanings that are active in those discursive practices, with special attention being paid to folk conceptions of communication itself, and the deeper meanings about being, relating, feeling, and dwelling that are associated with those practices.

3. For a sampling of a related body of work on environmental communication, see Cantrill (1993), the essays in Cantrill and Oravec (1996), Lange (1993), and Peterson (1997). Similarly, I have explored the dueling discourses that activate a land-use dispute in Western Massachusetts (Carbaugh, 1996b, pp. 157–190), and with Karen Wolf another concerning Anglos and Apaches in Arizona (Carbaugh & Wolf, 1999).

4. My use of the *dwelling* concept is informed by Heidegger (1971, 1977), and used by Ingold (1992), as well as Feld and Basso (1996, pp. 3–11).

5. The name, Two Bears, is a pseudonym, as is Rising Wolf and Slow Talker. I use these pseudonyms to honor the commitments I have made during the course of these studies.

6. In terms of Searle's speech act theory, the illocutionary force at work here, when "listening" is explicitly mentioned, is partly at least, representational; with the point of the utterance (e.g., "if you sit and listen patiently") being to describe, however briefly, an action, to fit words about that action to a presumed cultural and physical world, to express a belief that the act is a potent way to be in that world, and to presume an extra-linguistic ethos of Blackfeet life for the realization of the act being so represented. This reading leans most heavily on dimensions 1, 2, 3, 4, and 10 in Searle's explication of illocutionary force (see Searle, 1990, pp. 350–355). The illocutionary force is also, at times, a moderate directive (e.g., "just listen"), inviting the hearer to do the very act of listening represented. Further, related reflections on the relation between listening in silence and speaking about silence appear in Bilmes (1994).

7. A Native American reader of the chapter made this observation, which delighted me no end. "I believe, and this may be different from Two Bears, that wherever I 'listen' in this great land, must have sacredness, in the respect that the ancestors lived everywhere on this land and the world and all its creatures are sacred. But as Awiakta, the Cherokee poet, writer, and activist has said it is difficult to 'listen' through concrete." Indeed!

8. Also, as is evident in Blackfeet history (e.g., see Bullchild, 1985) and novels (e.g., see Welch, 1987a, 1987b) and various occasions of storytelling, this access has diminished with the coming of "the modern-day world," this latter phrase often operating as a code phrase meaning, "the Whiteman's world."

9. The superb novel *Fools Crow*, by Blackfeet author, James Welch (1987), contains several dialogues between Blackfeet and animals. For a sustained example, see the dialogue between the raven, a "power animal" of a healer, the healer, and the title character. In the dialogue, raven and Fools Crow show their ability to speak and interact with each other through a shared universal language (pp. 46–58).

10. Note that the "listening" form can work in ways both mundane, and, mysterious. For the latter, I am quite influenced by Two Bears', Rising Wolf's, and many others' stories about the possible mysteries created and unveiled through the form. Also, I am influenced by the late Blackfeet elder and author, Percy Bullchild (1985), who discussed—especially through the Scarface myth—various surprising ways a spirit can make itself known and "give you its powers of mystery" (pp. 325–390; see also Welch 1987).

11. I have explored these events and their history through the narrative form (Carbaugh, 2001).

12. The interpretive procedure has been summarized elsewhere and applied in a variety of essays (e.g., Carbaugh, 1996b; Fitch, 1998; Hall & Valde, 1995; Philipsen, 1992).

↤ 8 ↦

"The Passing Occasion and the Long Story":[1]
Four Cultural Conversations

In chapter 1, I introduced a complex thesis about conversation as a practice, a practice that says something not only about communicative action itself, but also about ways of relating, feeling, being, and dwelling in nature. In the intervening chapters, I have illustrated this thesis by presenting descriptions of specific communication practices as well as interpretations of those practices. The interpretations showed how cultural conversations operate as specific means of organizing communicative actions. Each at times conveyed rich messages about social relationships, about the role of emotion in participants' lives, about identities at play, and about the modes of emplaced living involved in the performance. In this final chapter, I discuss some general conclusions based on this approach to communication as it applies in these and other, related studies. Specifically, I summarize some of the key cultural features in the four expressive systems discussed in the book, with special attention to the thesis that communication can be understood as a complex metacultural commentary about ways of being, acting, feeling, relating, and dwelling. Eventually, I explicate some propositions of the general investigative stance that was used to generate these studies of cultural premises in practices of conversation.

FOUR DISCURSIVE CODES:
OF "SELF," "SILENCE," "SOUL,"AND "SPIRIT"

Each of the four cultural conversations explored in this book can be summarized generally by discussing a rich cultural symbol, a form of communicative action, the motivational unit these make particularly relevant, and the premises created and presumed by this symbol, form, and motivational theme. I briefly summarize parts of each expressive system, as such, in an effort to capture a deep discursive code through which that distinctive conversational practice is being cast. In the process, I allude to the larger symbolic meanings at play when conversation is being so conducted. Treating conversation as a symbolic resource is thus one way of tying "larger cultural stories to the passing occasions of conversation," of saying something about participants' enduring premises as these are immanent in various parts of a cultural conversation.

USAmerican "Self" Expression

The symbol of "self"—as conceived and used in a popular USAmerican discourse—draws attention to the unique and enduring qualities of individuals. In its use, and celebration, people are cast, presumably, as individuals with their own thoughts, feelings, and experiences. Because these thoughts, feelings, and experiences are believed to be uniquely within each person, acts of communication are required that make them public. A principal and necessary act, then, is disclosing factually about oneself. This act aims to reveal what one thinks about matters at hand, and what one thinks—the thoughts or feelings one has—is presumably, to a large degree, unique to the person as an individual. For this reason, it is crucial to hear from him, her, and every one of us. People are told, from this stance, to express "self" freely, for this is a fundamental right, protected by institutions of law and championed in the folk's morality. In brief, the symbol, "self," the form of speaking factually, the topics of individual thoughts, feelings, and experiences, and the motivational theme and right to so speak, create a form of self-expression that is distinct and prominent in some scenes of USAmerican life.

That one should speak and act on the basis of one's individuality, and forge relations accordingly, was apparent in an English pub as an American spoke freely about his interests and social relationships, in a Finnish lecture as an American academic tried to get the Finnish audience speaking freely partly by using their personal names, in a meeting between USAmerican and Russian professors as the American academics talked about their problems, in talk shows as American hosts asked Russians to express themselves freely, or elsewhere when asking Finns about conversing on a bus, in meetings between a teacher and Native American students when the teacher expected students to speak openly and publicly, and in meetings between an ethnographer and his consultants, all of whom, at crucial times, practiced communication through different cultural codes. Beliefs that one can and should simply say what is on one's mind, do so in an unencumbered way, forge relations on these bases, feeling as if we all are "on the same page," so to speak, all belie the fact of difference; for even if somehow we are momentarily on the same page, the pages can quickly turn—into different books.

Making this USAmerican symbol, form, and motive explicit, helps us understand the expectation—that one practice communication as a self who speaks factually about one's individual thoughts, feelings, and experiences, and that one do so freely. The expectation is, to some degree, largely a cultural one, one among many possible others. A dimension of meaning runs through this system: *One is (and should be) an expressive individual, who communicates openly, and expresses feelings freely.* These premises for being a person become part of a taken-for-granted consensus about conversation as it is practiced in this cultural way. The fundamental moral unit is personal, one's self, and it is to be expressed in an open and free way. Acts that hide the self, or amplify other concerns—such as silent messages, collective virtues, or spiritual attentiveness—can feel suspicious, or somehow not quite right, from the vantage of this expressive practice. If left inscrutable, the expressive system—this symbol, form, motives, and premises—can easily supplant and negatively connote other selves it seeks to understand (see, e.g., Chick, 1990; R. Scollon & S. Scollon, 1981).

Finnish "Silence" (Quietude or *Hiljaisus*)

The symbol of "silence" (or, in Finnish, *hiljaisus*) draws attention to kinds of interactional occasions that some Finnish people create and produce together. In these moments, when silence is being practiced together, this act can convey respect for those present, a preference for a reserved attitude concerning talk, and deference to a nonverbal co-presence among people as an important and natural form of social action. Because silent action is, at times, presumably "a natural way to be" (in Finnish, *luonteva tapa olla*), talking can seem, in those times, less natural, even unnatural. Like fine wine, on these occasions verbal communication is to be used sparingly and, when done, done thoughtfully, as fitting for the occasion. Proper talk, in public, should be worthy of others' attention, about something not obvious to others, in a typically nonconflictual, nor contentious way, and, as such, can form important and enduring links between people. Principal and prominent acts, from this view, are social silence and speaking thoughtfully. This provides a valuable orientation that honors each others' natural desire to be unimpeded, and relatively free from the considerable impositions of a verbal realm. People are told through this code to be attentive to others and be respectful of them, and when speaking to be sure you have something socially worthwhile to say. In brief, the symbol of silence, the form of "care-full" and thoughtful speech, the topic of worthy social commentary, and the motivational theme to stay silent unless having something important to say, create a form of communication practice that is prominent and important in some scenes of Finnish life.

That one should give others the time and space to reflect, that one should do so on one's own, and forge relations accordingly was apparent in greetings between a Finn and some Americans, in complimenting the baker of freshly baked bread, in third-party introductions between Finnish and American academics, and in styles of public discourse, including ways Finnish speakers talked with an American correspondent about being Finnish. Beliefs that we can and should carefully watch what is going on around us, give people their own space and time, and respect the social scene so set, all give a special place to "silence" and quietude in social life, as well as the premises about the person it presumes and creates.

Making this symbol, these modes and motives of practice explicit, helps us understand an urge to quietude as a cultural one. Dimensions of meaning of course run through this expressive system as well, *for it presumes a particular model for the person: Speak when one has something to say that is worthy of others' consideration. Otherwise, defer to others by being a silent, respectful, and reserved person; be one who can and should watch and listen, rather than being engaged in needless chatter*. These premises for being a person are part of an unspoken consensus that is practiced in a cultural way. The fundamental unit is a socially active one, a respectful way of being together in which silence and sparse expression can—and should, at least occasionally—be honored and valued.

Russian "Soul Talk" (or, in Russian, *Razgovor Po Dusham*)

The symbol of *soul* draws attention to a quality of persons and speaking that is infused with proper feeling and action. This is understood to go deeper than the normal course of daily routines, and typically applies to non-political domains. When active in conversation, "soul talk" involves a deeper morality of a common life, a transcendental quality of humanness, with this being predicated to a collective agent. Soul talk is thus valorized as a form of conversational practice, responds to social difficulties and ills, and is most fitting to intimate occasions where "good relations" are present (in Russian, *vzaimootnoshenia*). The practice is also possibly done with less intimate others who can converse as an open and accepting "soul" (in Russian, *raspolagaet*). Principal and prominent acts of this sort create deeply felt and morally charged ideas about human situations and nature, as collective virtues about good living are being not only applied, but challenged and negotiated. This provides a way of honoring a common and pervasive quality in human beings that orients people to shared moral premises for living. In soul talk, people are expected to give each other the special kind of attention that permits "the union of souls" as part of common virtuous living. In brief, the symbol of soul, the practice of espousing deep feelings about life's challenges and problems, the topic of one's life and collective morality, the motivational demand to respect and understand others while helping them judge what is good living, create a form of practice that is prominent in many scenes of Russian life.

That one should produce and interpret some parts of conversation as matters of a personal and collective morality, that one expects others to do the same, and that social relations can and should be forged accordingly, was apparent in meetings between Russian and USAmerican academics, between Russian students and USAmerican teachers, and in discussions between a USAmerican talk-show host and Russian teens. Beliefs that social and personal difficulties can be addressed through soulfelt expressions, that people can help each other by listening and giving counsel along these lines, and that proper social living is enhanced by doing so, all give a special place to soul as part and parcel of a distinctively Russian conversation, and the model person it presumes and creates.

Making this symbol, form of practice, and motivational theme explicit, helps us understand some of the cultural premises for speaking this way, about virtues, rather than another, for example, about facts. Dimensions of meaning of course run through this expressive system and say something not only about speaking, but about the person who so speaks: *A person has a body and a soul, and one cannot see but one can feel the soul; because of the soul, things can happen in and among persons that cannot happen in anything other than persons; these things can be good or bad; because of this part, a person can feel things that nothing other than persons can feel.* These premises for being a person are part of a deeply felt and dynamically integrative Russian cultural conversation. Within it, a fundamental discursive unit is made, a uniquely human and deeply moral one, a proper way of doing things in which soulful expression can and should be conducted and valued (Wierzbicka, 1989).

Blackfeet "Spirit" (in Blackfeet, *Atsimma'siwa or Waato'si*)

The Blackfeet symbol of *spirit* draws attention to an integral and real part of people, places, and things. This is something everpresent in the social and natural world, and because of this, it is something significant and important to monitor and acknowledge. Specific acts of communication are necessary in order to become attuned to this spiritual dimension of life, "listening" being principal among them. When listening in a distinctively Blackfeet way, one is conducting a cultural form of practice. This action of listening is specially relevant in particular places, is, in some sense, of those places, attends to them in particular ways, and links people to them in ways that orient to their special spiritual offerings. For this reason, it is crucial for people to listen accordingly. People are told that they need to listen, for this makes available to them certain agents and messages about life that are unavailable through other symbolic forms. The symbol of spirit, the form of listening, the topics of lessons for living, and the motivational desire to learn to live a full life all create a form of spiritual practice that is distinct in some scenes of Blackfeet life.

That one should listen accordingly, expect others to do the same, and thereby honor the full range of qualities—the spiritual and natural dimensions—in life, and that social relations should be so forged, at times, was apparent in a classroom between a USAmerican professor and Native American students, in conversations between a "Whiteman" and Blackfeet speakers, in different orientations to places and agents by Blackfeet and a "Whiteman," and in various discussions between "Whitemen" and Blackfeet about their places. Beliefs that lessons about living can be learned through a special version of listening, that people can help themselves, others, and their places through this practice, and that proper living in place, or dwelling, involves such a practice, all give a special place to spiritual listening, thus making it a particularly rich part of a Blackfeet conversation, and person.

Making this symbol, form of practice, and motivational themes explicit, helps us understand specific cultural premises for listening, at times, rather than speaking. Dimensions of meaning run through this expressive system, saying something deeply about being, acting, feeling, and dwelling: *Things, people, animals, and places are interconnected in ways that are knowable, and unknowable; Spirits exist in things, people, animals, and places. People can and should listen to this world; By listening, people can become attuned to this world; Becoming attuned to this is good.* These premises about the world, for acting within it, for feeling about it, all are expressively active in parts of a Blackfeet cultural conversation. Through it, a fundamental discursive unit is deeply situated, providing a proper way of doing things in their proper places, becoming attuned to the spirit expressing itself, and learning from it, as a lesson in living.

CULTURAL CONVERSATIONS AND DISCOURSES: SHARED IDENTITY, COMMUNICATION PRACTICE, AND PREMISES OF PERSONHOOD

The theory of cultural communication was first presented by Gerry Philipsen at a conference on communication theory in Yugoslavia in 1980. In the first published version of that theory, he conceived a principal function of communication to be a cultural one, that is, "the creation, affirmation, and negotiation of shared identity" (Philipsen, 1987, p. 279). In this sense, cultural communication can be understood as an approach to investigating the premises and practices of shared identity as these are active in conversation and cultural life. *One focal dimension, then, in cultural conversations is the presumption and expression of shared identity, that is, the expressive orientation of interactants to a common social and cultural life.* Philipsen (1989; see also 2002) summarized and reviewed this dimension of communication as a process of *membering*, bringing into view the parts of social interaction that alert and connect people to their common ways of living together.

There are, of course, various ways of understanding communication as a cultural phenomenon. One can posit participants' beliefs about it that are special, notice styles of enactment that are distinctive in one community more than another, or analyze a range of practices that are active within a community's scenes. The theory of cultural communication formulates these more specifically, from the vantage of three concerns: (a) the structuring of shared identity in *codes*, (b) the processual enactment of this structuring in *conversations*, and (c) the group context of these structuring processes in *community*. Three ways of conceptualizing the communication of shared identity are thus explicated in the theory, in terms of its *structure* in codes, its *process* in conversation, and its *context* in community. The special focus in the preceding studies has been on the second of these, the processual enactment of cultural codes in conversation, interpreting this from the point of view of the interactants' codes. By exploring acts within conversational sequences, and these as parts of expressive systems, the studies have brought to the fore *cultural conversations*, the processual creation, use, and negotiation of interactants' codes in ongoing, social interaction.

The case studies in this book focused on moments in conversation when a processual enactment of the communal function is getting done, highlighting social interactional processes in which "membering" is accomplished. Kept in the fore has been the enactment of shared identity, a collective sense of who we are that is presumed and valorized in specific communication practices. *Shared identity*

becomes active through particular kinds of communication prac-
tices that are deemed prominent, accessible, and important to a
people, these being situated in social conversations as declarations
of "a way we are, and, the way we do things around here." For some,
the feeling is we can (and should) speak our individual minds, express
our selves, thoughts, and feelings in unencumbered ways; for some,
the feeling is we can (and should) keep our selves properly under
wraps, a source for contemplation and thought, and thus not engage in
needless talk; for some, the feeling is we can (and should) speak our
collective virtue, expressing the moral imperatives we as a people presumably believe; for some, we can (and should) listen to the natural
and human world express itself, for this is a source of deep spiritual
wisdom that helps us live the good life every day. Each peopled place
valorizes some communication practice as these, sometimes doing so
quite contentiously, and thus each crafts and molds its codes to the
specific demands of conversational occasions.

Communication practices as these can be understood as patterns of
message endowed action and their meanings (Carbaugh, Gibson, &
Milburn, 1995). Whether one speaks or is silent, whether one speaks
about one's self or one's collective virtues, or whether one speaks or
listens, all involve doing one kind of practice rather than others.
Clearly all such acts can be done, to one degree or another by any of us.
But, each is not conceived, valorized, nor elaborated in practice in all
expressive systems nor all social contexts in the same ways. As a result, each needs to be discovered and understood in its own right, in its
own interactional context, as part of its own expressive system, for the
work it gets done.

Part of the task in the previous studies has consisted, then, first, *in*
noticing, or discovering (this taking a considerable amount of time in
some cases), then *recording* communication practices that are
deemed significant and important to interlocutors. As mentioned in
the introduction to the book, this task has involved a kind of technical,
descriptive analysis of social interaction, seeking to present moments
of conversations "in their own right." This effort grounds the studies in
actual conversational practices that participants have created together, in their ways of speaking to and/or about each other.

This primary task has involved noticing that a practice is indeed active—silence can be easily missed by those from a "talking culture"—recording the practice as something worthy in its own right,
and then characterizing what the practice indeed is. *This process of*
noticing, recording, and characterizing cultural conversations
draws attention to communication practice as something inter-
actionally improvised through acts in sequences, and moreover, as
something deeply meaningful to participants. A question from an

Englishman to an American at a pub in England, from a Finnish man to an American during an introduction in Finland, from an American to a Russian during a talk show in Russia, or about a crow—or a public speech—by a northern Plains Indian, all exhibit practices, with these practices being intimately tied to cultural ways of practicing conversational life. Yet we often deny the local and particular character in our own and others' practices, not hearing, fully, from whence we are "speaking." Noticing, recording, and characterizing communication practices as cast in cultural conversations, as endowed with cultural messages, as somehow tied to local ways of living, is one effort to understand the cultural life of conversation, as reflecting interactants' premises for living.

Getting at the full and deep meanings of communication practices—if this is at all possible—presents a challenging interpretive task. We pose the question: What must be presumed—believed and/or valued—in order for that contribution to the conversation to be indeed what it is for these participants? In response to the question, I have formulated throughout cultural premises about interactional moments that are active in conversation. The claim I make is that these are literally, *in* the conversational moves of concern, with these premises being—according to the argument—what is "said"—in Ricouer's and Geertz's senses—in the practice. In other words, *cultural premises are formulations of the meanings in the conversational uses of codes, with these formulations capturing how participants' beliefs about being, acting, feeling, relating, and dwelling in place are inextricably woven into the momentary fabric of social interactional life.*

The formulation of cultural premises as active in conversation has followed a systematic set of commitments that can be made explicit in a series of propositions. *A proposition about descriptive inquiry: Conversation is a practice that can and should be described on its own, in its own right, while attentive to its discursive codes.* This commitment has involved technical, descriptive analyses of acts in sequences, evident mostly in transcriptions. From my point of view, these are "eventual formulations," for they reflect both the conversational practice being investigated, as well as findings about the practice so investigated. Whether a "lip smack" is relevant to document, or a co-present silence before an initial turn of speaking, and so on, depends on the eventual meaningfulness of such communicative acts and interactions to participants. The descriptive analysis, the moments of talk eventually recorded on paper, thus reflect both conversation in its own right, and its significance to those who produced it, in the first instance. Descriptive analyses of talk thus, inevitably, reflect shared conceptions of conversational practice, whether analysts' and/or participants', the latter being of central concern to us here.

Coming to understand indeed what was produced in conversation, at least as explored here, is a product of interpretive inquiry as well. That procedure has followed a systematic process erected upon a *general proposition about interpretive inquiry: Communication, conversation and social interaction involves a complex metacultural commentary, explicitly and/or implicitly, about identities, actions, feelings, relations, and living in place.* As people engage in practices of communication, so they produce and monitor who they are, what they are doing together, how they feel about what is going on, how they are related, and how they inhabit places. Although in any one practice, all features of this commentary are not equally relevant, each is potentially salient for interpreting the cultural significance and sense of the practice getting done. Asking about each, in turn, provides a systematic way of "reading" or interpreting the meanings in the practice. Each suggests dimensions of potential significance for understanding what is getting done. Each can be expressed explicitly or more implicitly, and known as part of the common understanding in the communal conversation, as such. Let us briefly look at each.

The five interpretive dimensions of this theory have been shown to be relevant and salient in different ways in various cultural conversations. Each has been, and further can be explored by posing a question. To begin, we can ask, in this practice of communication, through this discourse, who are we presumed or presented to be? *Corollary one: Conversation is a metacultural commentary about being, and identity, with messages about who we are—and should be—being coded into this practice of conversation.* How is this so? Part of the interpretive work in the analysis of cultural conversation is the hearing of messages about shared identity in social interaction. Formulating premises about identity and being, making explicit the taken-for-granted understandings for the structuring of talk as such helps us understand part of its significance to interlocutors. It helps us understand some of the work the acts both presume, and re-create in their enactment, these being attached to a sense of "who we are." Participants' sometimes have a strong sense that we structure the conversation one way when being one kind of person, and another way when being another. This can be captured and rendered by interpreting conversation thusly. This is evident when a community of speakers, on one occasion, enacts "time" in a Puerto Rican way, thus identifying themselves as "Puerto Rican," yet also the same speakers construct "time" differently in other conversational occasions, in ways deemed "more efficient" and desirable, such as in settings of U.S. business (Milburn, 2000). From the vantage of an individual, one multicultural speaker may structure conversation differently depending on the desired affiliation the occasion makes relevant (Hastings, 2000; Yep,

1998). In each, conversation is being cast and conducted in a way that presumes a way of being, or ways of being, in a moment of talk, an experience of communal identity.

A second kind of interpretive question can yield beliefs and values about action that are immanent in conversational practices. We ask: In this practice of communication, what are we doing, and what should we be doing? *Corollary two: Conversation is a metacultural commentary about acting, with messages about what we are doing, and should be doing, being coded into the practice of conversation.* As conversation flows along, so do participants' senses of what they are doing together, of when they have completed one kind of activity and moved to another, or of what should be getting done. Whether we should be silently co-present, verbally engaged, and if verbally engaged, in a self-expressive or soulful way, for example, is part of what is monitored and understood in the practice of conversation. Coming to understand messages as these, about action, can help us interpret cultural lives in conversation. Such inquiry helps us understand the cultural status of action and meanings, and whether, for example, saying "I'm sorry," is heard from a U.S. view as a sincere admission of responsibility, or whether from a Japanese view as a common discrepancy between what is said and one's inner feelings (Kotani, 2002). Exploring the messages about action in conversational practices helps us understand the status of those actions as cultural practices.

A third interpretive question can be posed: How do we feel about this practice of communication, in and about which we are engaged? *Corollary three: Conversation is a metacultural commentary about emotion, with messages about how we feel—and should feel—being coded into acts of conversation.* How a conversation is "keyed" (Hymes, 1972), the feeling it expresses, or invokes, and whether this is a shared feeling or not, all can be understood as part of a conversational activity. The "object" of feeling, or what one feels about, is sometimes crucially significant to understand as well, for how one feels about the activity getting done, or the opinion of another, or about the cawing of a crow, or about the collective morality of one's people, and so on; all are objects of possible feeling. How one feels, about what, with what intensity, all become part of the conversational commentary, explicit or not, that is, the ongoing flow of cultural and conversational life (cf. Kotani, 2002; Scruton, 1979).

How are we being related in this practice of communication? *Corollary four: Conversation is a metacultural commentary about relating, with messages about social relations being coded into acts of conversation.* Acts of conversation of course can presume, and/or relate people in particular ways. Kristine Fitch (1998) explored this feature of Colombian conversation with the idea that it creatively presupposes an "interpersonal ideology," that is, "a subset of cultural premises related most specifically to interpersonal relationships" (p. 182). How is it that specific conversational practices relate us, one to another? Some USAmerican acts of communicating and sharing feelings presume a union of intimates (Carbaugh, 1988b; Katriel & Philipsen, 1981); some Russian acts of "soul talk" presume a relation of solidarity (Khatskevich, 2002); "introductions" presume movement along relational dimensions; "listening" presumes a kindred relation with that which surrounds one. In conversation and social interaction are messages about how people are related to each other and the world around them. Formulating these relations as premises, and understanding how these premises are active in practice, helps us understand some of the cultural life in conversation.

A fifth interpretive question can be posed: How does this communication relate us to places? *Corollary five: Conversation is a metacultural commentary about dwelling, with messages about living in place being coded into acts of conversation.* Where are we, and how are we related to this place? Communication, conversation and social interaction provide people senses of places, and their place within them. Tracking how this is done through moments of talk provides a way of understanding both the place of talk in people's lives, and the talk of place as part of conversation and cultural life. In this sense, a Blackfeet form of listening presumes a particular conception of the world and one's place within it; soul talk presumes a particular sense of persons and the cosmos of which they are part; self-talk says something about the separation of people from each other and their environment; and silent co-presence says something about the importance of watching the world one inhabits and understanding one's place always as a limited part of it. A deep reading of conversational practice may reveal something relevant, perhaps even salient about dwelling as a meaning in conversational practice (Feld & Basso, 1996). If so, this can help us understand the cultural life in conversation.

These five probes—these dimensions in cultural discourses—can be used to interpret the meaningfulness of conversation to participants. By formulating a system of premises about each that is relevant, and locating these in specific conversational practices, we can create deeper readings about conversation, as a message-endowed practice, as a working of codes in conversation (Carbaugh, 1988b, 1996b; Philipsen, 1987). Adding these interpretations to the technical and detailed descriptions of conversational practices will help us understand what is at stake as people talk, what they presume their talk to be, and what they are making of themselves and their worlds in this process. Certainly not all features are always relevant in each such practice, but any one might be central to any one practice, with the larger set together providing a richly systematic way of interpreting cultural conversations as a deeply coded activity.

The cultural premises of main concern in these studies have been the premises about conversational activity, unveiling in each case a kind of cultural philosophy of communication. These have been shown as intimately tied to others, premises of personhood in particular. With these, I have formulated two things: the basic beliefs about the action getting done in a particular kind of communication practice; and further, how these premises are inextricably tied to premises of personhood, both being understood, in a real sense, as in conversational practice. Ways of using a language are thus being understood as inevitably tied to ways of being a person (Rosaldo, 1982).

In concluding, it is important, again, to emphasize that these premises are, therefore, fundamentally about *practices* that people have created, and thus are not tied in any deterministic way to "a people" or a geographic region, and so forth. Any one particularly skilled multicultural person may speak, or be, in multiple ways. In turn, any particular American, or Finn, or Blackfoot, or Russian may dislike or disown any one particular practice associated with "his people or place." However, if these studies are in some sense valid, one could not say there is no such thing as a practice of the Russian "soul," or a Finnish practice of quietude and "silence," or a USAmerican practice of expressing one's "self," or a Blackfeet practice of "listening" in a particular way. Such practices may or may not be appreciated by any one person, may or may not appear in any one occasion, yet still be active in some social ways—with common meanings—in some scenes of cultural life. In this sense, the claims being made are about cultural features in conversational practices, their meanings in contexts, when they are active, not about people and their turns of mind. Premises of communication and personhood, then, in this sense, refer primarily to dimensions and meanings of particular conversational practices, as these are momentarily active in particular acts in sequences. It is cultures in conversation that has been our main concern. Making these practices more scrutable should help us understand from whence we and others are speaking, from the views of the participants, thus honoring not only their meanings, but the practices through which they creatively live, on their own, and together with others.

ENDNOTE

1. This phrase is extracted from Clifford Geertz (1995) where he discusses understanding cultures as a "relation between the large and the little" (p. 50), movement from the little moments of conversation to the large contexts each such conversation presupposes and helps to create, and back again (both culturally and theoretically). This process is part of the main theme in the comparative analyses that comprise this book.

References

Agar, M. (1994). *Language shock: Understanding the culture of conversation.* New York: William Morrow & Co.

Auer-Rizzi, W., & Berry, M. (2000). Business vs. Cultural frames of reference in group decision making: interactions among Austrian, Finnish, and Swedish business students. *The Journal of Business Communication, 37,* 264–292.

Bailey, B. (2000). Communicative behavior and conflict between African-American customers and Korean immigrant retailers in Los Angeles, *Discourse & Society, 11,* 86–108.

Basso, K. (1979). *Portraits of "the Whiteman": Linguistic play and cultural symbols among the western Apache.* Cambridge, England: Cambridge University Press.

Basso, K. (1990). *Western Apache language and culture.* Tucson: University of Arizona Press.

Basso, K. (1996). *Wisdom sits in places: Landscape and language among the western Apache.* Albuquerque, NM: University of New Mexico Press.

Bauman, R.. (1970). Aspects of 17th century Quaker rhetoric. *Quarterly Journal of Speech, 56,* 67–74.

Bauman, R. (1986). *Story, performance, and event: Contextual studies of oral narrative.* Cambridge, England: Cambridge University Press.

Bauman, R., & Sherzer, J. (1990). Introduction. In R. Bauman & J. Sherzer (Eds.), *Explorations in the ethnography of speaking.* Cambridge, England: Cambridge University Press.

Baxter, L. (1993). "Talking things through" and "putting it in writing": Two codes of communication in an academic institution. *Journal of Applied Communication Research, 21,* 313–326.

Baxter, L., & Goldsmith, D. (1990). Cultural terms for communication events among some American high school adolescents. *Western Journal of Speech Communication, 54,* 377–394.

Berry, M. (1997). Speaking culturally about personhood, motherhood, and career. *Administrative Studies [Finland], 4,* 304–325.

Berry, W. (1990). *What are people for?* San Francisco: North Point Press.

Billig, M., & Schegloff, E. (1999). Critical discourse analysis and conversation analysis. *Discourse & Society, 10,* 543–587.

Bilmes, J. (1994). Constituting silence: Life in the world of total meaning. *Semiotica, 98,* 73–87.

Bitzer, L. (1968). The rhetorical situation. *Philosophy and Rhetoric, 1,* 1–14.

Bloch, L.-R. (2003). Who's afraid of being a *friere?* The analysis of communication through a key cultural frame. *Communication Theory, 13,* 125–159.

Blommaert, J. (1998). Different approaches to intercultural communication: A critical survey. Plenary lecture, Lernen und Arbeiten in einer international vernetzten und multikulturellen Gesellschaft, Expertentagung Universitat Bremen, Institut fur Projektmanagement und Witschaftsinformatik [Learning and working in an internationally interlaced and multicultural society, expert conference University of Bremen, Institute for Project Management] (IPMI), 27–28 February.

Bordewich, F. (1996). *Killing the White man's Indian: Reinventing Native Americans at the end of the twentieth century.* New York: Doubleday.

Bradley, J. H. (1923). *Characteristics, habits, and customs of the Black-feet Indian* (V. 16). Contributions to the Historical Society of Montana.

Braithwaite, Charles. (1997). Sa'ah naaghai bik'eh hozhoon [Navajo philosophy for living]: An ethnography of Navajo educational communication practices. *Communication Education, 46,* 219–233.

Briggs, C. (1986). *Learning how to ask: A sociolinguistic appraisal of the role of the interview in social science research.* Cambridge, England: Cambridge University Press.

Brockmeier, J., & Carbaugh, D. (Eds.). (2001). *Narrative and identity: Studies in autobiography, self, and culture.* Amsterdam/Philadelphia: J. J. Benjamins.

Bryan, Jr., W. (1985). *Montana's Indians: Yesterday and today.* Helena, MT: Montana Magazine, Inc.

Bullchild, P. (1985). *The sun came down: The history of the world as my Blackfeet Elders told it.* San Francisco: Harper & Row.

Burke, K. (1965). *Permanence and change.* Indianapolis: Bobbs-Merrill.

Cameron, D. (1995). *Verbal hygiene.* London & New York: Routledge.

Cameron, D. (2000). *Good to talk?: Living and working in a communication culture.* London, Thousand Oaks, and New Delhi: Sage.

Cantrill, J. (1993). Communication and our environment: Categorizing research in environmental advocacy. *Journal of Applied Communication Research, 21,* 66–95.

Cantrill, J., & Oravec, C. (Eds.). (1996). *The symbolic earth: Discourse and our creation of the environment.* Lexington: University of Kentucky Press.

Carbaugh, D. (1987). Communication rules in DONAHUE discourse. *Research on Language and Social Interaction, 21,* 31–62.

Carbaugh, D. (1988a). Comments on "culture" in communication inquiry. *Communication Reports, 1,* 38–41.

Carbaugh, D. (1988b). *Talking American: Cultural discourses on DONAHUE.* Norwood, NJ: Ablex.

Carbaugh, D. (1988/1989). Deep agony: "Self" vs. "society" in DONAHUE discourse. *Research on Language and Social Interaction, 22,* 179–212.

Carbaugh, D. (1989). Fifty terms for talk: A cross-cultural study. *International and Intercultural Communication Annual, 13,* 93–120.

Carbaugh, D. (Ed.). (1990a). *Cultural communication and intercultural contact.* Hillsdale, NJ: Lawrence Erlbaum Associates.

Carbaugh, D. (1990b). Intercultural communication. In D. Carbaugh (Ed.), *Cultural communication and intercultural contact* (pp. 151–175). Hillsdale, NJ: Lawrence Erlbaum Associates.

Carbaugh, D. (1990c). Toward a perspective on cultural communication and intercultural contact. *Semiotica, 80,* 15–35.

Carbaugh, D. (1993a). Communication competence and cultural pragmatics: Reflections on Soviet and American encounters. *International and Intercultural Communication Annual, 17,* 168–183.

Carbaugh, D. (1993b). Cultural pragmatics and intercultural competence. In L. Lofman, L. Kurki-Suonio, S. Pellinen, & J. Lehtonen (Eds.), *The competent intercultural communicator AFinLA yearbook 1993, No. 51,* 117–129.

Carbaugh, D. (1993c). "Soul" and "self": Soviet and American cultures in conversation. *Quarterly Journal of Speech, 79,* 182–200.

Carbaugh, D. (1994a). Are Americans really superficial?: Notes on Finnish and American Cultures in linguistic action. In L. Salo (toim./ed.), *Kieli and Kulttuuri oppimisessa* [Language and culture in teaching and learning] (pp. 53–60), Publications of the Department of Communication, University of Jyvaskyla, Finland, 1995; Reprinted in the Finnish journal *Tempus, 4,* 1995, 6–9; and in L. Samovar & R. Porter (Eds.), *Intercultural communication: A reader* (8th ed.). Wadsworth.

Carbaugh, D. (1994b). Cultures in conversation: Prospects for new world communities. In D. Marsh & L. Salo-Lee (Eds.), *Europe on the move: Fusion or fission* (pp. 24–34). University of Jyväsklä and SIETAREuropa.

Carbaugh, D. (1995). The ethnographic theory of Philipsen and Associates. In D. Cushman & B. Kovacic (Eds.), *Watershed theories of human communication.* Albany, NY: State University of New York Press.

Carbaugh, D. (1996a). Naturalizing communication and culture. In J. Cantrill and C. Oravec (Eds.), *The symbolic earth: Discourse and our creation of the environment* (pp. 38–57). Lexington: University of Kentucky Press.

Carbaugh, D. (1996b). *Situating selves: The communication of social identities in American scenes.* Albany, NY: State University of New York Press.

Carbaugh, D. (2001). "The people will come to you": Blackfeet narrative as a resource for contemporary living. In J. Brockmeier & D. Carbaugh (Eds.), *Narrative and identity: Studies in autobiography, self, and culture* (pp. 103–127). Amsterdam/Philadelphia: J. J. Benjamins.

Carbaugh, D. (2002). Some distinctive features of USAmerican conversation. In W. Eadie & P. Nelson (Eds.), *The changing conversation in America* (pp. 61–75). Thousand Oaks, CA: Sage.

Carbaugh, D., Gibson, T., & Milburn, T. A. (1997). A view of communication and culture: Scenes in an ethnic cultural center and private college. In B. Kovacic (Ed.), *Emerging theories of human communication* (pp. 1–24). Albany, NY: State University of New York Press.

Carbaugh, D., & Hastings, S. (1992). A role for communication theory in ethnography and cultural analysis, *Communication Theory, 2,* 156–165.

Carbaugh, D., & Poutiainen, S. (2000). By way of introduction: An American and Finnish dialogue. In M. Lustig & J. Koester (Eds.), *Among US: Essays in identity, belonging, and intercultural competence* (pp. 203–212). New York: Addison & Wesley Longman.

Carbaugh, D., & Wolf, K. (1999). Situating rhetoric in cultural discourses. *International and Intercultural Communication Annual 22,* 19–30.

Chick, J. K. (1990). The interactional accomplishment of discrimination in South Africa. In D. Carbaugh (Ed.), *Cultural communication and intercultural contact* (pp. 225–252). Hillsdale, NJ: Lawrence Erlbaum Associates.

Chick, J. K. (1996). Intercultural communication. In S. L. Mckay & N. H. Hornberger (Eds.), *Sociolinguistics and language teaching* (pp. 329–348). Cambridge, England: Cambridge University Press.

Clements, W. M. (2002). *Oratory in native North America.* Tucson, AZ: University of Arizona Press.

Covarrubias, P. (2002). *Culture, communication, and cooperation: Interpersonal relations and pronominal address in a Mexican organization.* Lanham, MD: Rowan & Littlefield.

Craig, R. T. (1999a). Communication theory as a field. *Communication Theory, 9,* 119–161.

Craig, R. T. (1999b). Metadiscourse, theory, and practice. *Research on Language and Social Interaction, 32,* 21–29.

Daniel, J., & Smitherman, G. (1976). "How I got over": Communication dynamics in the Black community. *Quarterly Journal of Speech, 62,* 26–39.

Darnell, R. (1988). The implications of Cree interactional etiquette. In R. Darnell & M. Foster (Eds.), *Native North American interaction patterns* (pp. 69–77). Hull, Quebec: Canadian Museum of Civilization.

Deloria, Jr., V. (1991). Reflection and revelation: Knowing land, places and ourselves. In *The power of place: Sacred ground in natural and human environments* (pp. 28–40). Wheaton, IL: Quest Books.

Dempsey, H. A. (1972). *Crowfoot: Chief of the Blackfeet.* Norman, OK: University of Oklahoma Press.

Dempsey, H. A. (1994). *The amazing death of Calf Shirt and other Blackfoot stories: Three hundred years of Blackfoot history.* Saskatoon, Saskatchewan: Fifth House Publishers.

Ewers, J. C. (1958). *The Blackfeet: Raiders on the northwest plains.* Norman, OK: University of Oklahoma Press.

Feld, S., & Basso, K. (Eds.). (1996). *Senses of place*. Albuquerque, NM: University of New Mexico Press.

Fitch, K. (1991). The interplay of linguistic universals and cultural knowledge in personal address: Colombian *Madre* terms. *Communication Monographs, 58,* 254–272.

Fitch, K. (1994). A cross-cultural study of corrective sequences and some implications for compliance-gaining research. *Communication Monographs, 61,* 185–209.

Fitch, K. (1998). *Speaking relationally: Culture and interpersonal communication in Colombia*. New York: Guilford Press.

Flyvbjerg, B. (2001). *Making social science matter: Why social inquiry fails and how it can succeed again*. Cambridge, England: Cambridge University Press.

Foley, D. E. (1995). *The heartland chronicles*. Philadelphia, PA: University of Pennsylvania Press.

Frantz, D., & Russell, N. J. (1995). *Blackfoot dictionary of stems, roots, and affixes* (2nd ed.). Toronto: University of Toronto Press.

Gadamer, H. (1977). *Philosophical hermeneutics*. Berkeley: University of California Press.

Garrett, M. (1993). Wit, power, and oppositional groups: A case study of "pure talk." *Quarterly Journal of Speech, 79,* 303–318.

Geertz, C. (1973). *The interpretation of cultures*. New York: Basic Books.

Geertz, C. (1995). *After the fact: Two centuries, four decades, one anthropologist*. Cambridge & London: Harvard University Press.

Goffman, E.. (1967). *Interaction ritual: Essays on face-to-face behavior*. New York: Pantheon Books.

Goldfrank, E. (1945). *Changing configurations in the social organization of a Blackfoot tribe during the reserve period (the blood of Alberta, Canada)* (No. 8). Monographs of the American Ethnological Society (A. I. Hallowell, Ed.). New York: J. J. Augustin.

Griefat, Y., & Katriel, T. (1989). Life demands *Musayra*: Communication and culture among Arabs in Israel. *International and Intercultural Communication Annual, 13,* 121–138.

Grimshaw, A. (1992). Research on the discourse of international negotiations: A path to understanding international conflict processes. *Sociological Forum, 7,* 87–119.

Grinnell, G. B. (1962). *Blackfoot lodge tales*. Lincoln, NE: University of Nebraska Press.

Ground, M. (1978). *Grass woman stories*. Browning, MT: Blackfeet Heritage Program.

Gudykunst, W., & Ting-Toomey, S. (1988). *Culture and interpersonal communication*. Newbury Park, CA: Sage.

Gumperz, J. (1982). *Discourse strategies*. Cambridge, England: Cambridge University Press.

Gumperz, J. (1992). Interviewing in intercultural situations. In P. Drew & J. Heritage (Eds.), *Talk at work: Interaction in institutional settings* (pp. 302–327). Cambridge, England: Cambridge University Press.

Gumperz, J., & Levinson, S. (Eds.). (1996). *Rethinking linguistic relativity*. Cambridge, England: Cambridge University Press.

Hall, B. (1991). An elaboration of the structural possibilities for engaging in alignment episodes. *Communication Monographs, 58*, 79–100.

Hall, B., & Valde, K. (1995). "Brown nosing" as a cultural resource in American organizational speech. *Research on Language and Social Interaction, 28*, 131–150.

Harré, R. (1984). *Personal being*. Cambridge, MA: Harvard University Press.

Hastings, S. O. (2000). Asian Indian "self-suppression" and self-disclosure: Enactment and adaptation of cultural identity. *Journal of Language and Social Psychology, 19*, 85–109.

Hastings, S. O. (2001). Social drama as a site for the communal construction and management of Asian Indian "stranger" identity. *Research on Language and Social Interaction, 34*, 309–335.

Heidegger, M. (1971). *Poetry, language, thought*. New York: Harper & Row.

Heidegger, M. (1977). Building dwelling thinking. In D. Krell (Ed.), *Martin Heidegger: Basic writings* (pp. 319–339). New York: Harper & Row.

Hester, S., & Eglin, P. (1997). *Culture in action: Studies in membership categorization analysis*. New York: University Press of America.

Hofstede, G. (1980). *Culture's consequences*. Newbury Park, CA: Sage.

Hopper, R. (1988). Speech, for instance: The exemplar in studies of conversation. *Journal of Language and Social Psychology, 7*, 137–153.

Hungry Wolf, B. (1980). *The ways of my grandmothers*. New York: William Morrow & Co.

Hutchby, I. (1999). Rhetorical strategies in audience participation debates on radio and TV. *Research on Language and Social Interaction, 32*, 243–268.

Hymes, D. (1962). The ethnography of speaking. In T. Gladwin & W. Sturtevant (Eds.), *Anthropology and human behavior* (pp. 13–53). Washington, DC: Anthropological Society of Washington.

Hymes, D. (1972). Models of the interaction of language and social life. In J. Gumperz & D. Hymes (Eds.), *Directions in sociolinguistics: The ethnography of communication* (pp. 35–71). New York: Holt, Rinehart, & Winston.

Hymes, D. (1981). "In vain I tried to tell you": Essays in Native American ethnopoetics. Philadelphia, PA: University of Pennsylvania Press.

Hymes, D. (1986). The general epistle of James. *International Journal of the Sociology of Language, 62*, 75–103.

Hymes, D. (1996). *Ethnography, linguistics, narrative inequality: Toward an understanding of voice*. New York: Taylor & Francis.

Ingold, T. (1992). Culture and the perception of the environment. In E. Croll & D. Parkin (Eds.), *Bush base, forest farm: Culture, environment, and development* (pp. 39–56). London: Routledge.

Jackson, S. (1986). Building a case for claims about discourse structure. In D. Ellis (Ed.), *Contemporary issues in language and discourse processes* (pp. 129–147). Hillsdale, NJ: Lawrence Erlbaum Associates.

Jacobs, S. (1988). Evidence and inference in conversation analysis. In J. Anderson (Ed.), *Communication Yearbook 11* (pp. 433–443). Newbury Park, CA: Sage.

Kahlberg, S. (1987). West German and American interactional forms: One level of structured misunderstanding. *Theory, Culture, and Society, 4,* 603–618.

Katriel, T. (1991). *Communal webs: Communication and culture in contemporary Israel.* Albany, NY: State University of New York Press.

Katriel, T. (2004). *Dialogic moments: From soul talks to talk radio in Israeli culture.* Detroit, MI: Wayne State University Press.

Katriel, T., & Philipsen, G. (1981). "What we need is communication": "Communication" as a cultural category in some American speech. *Communication Monographs, 48,* 301–317.

Katriel, T., & Shenhar, A. (1990). Tower and stockade: Dialogic narration in Israeli settlement ethos. *Quarterly Journal of Speech, 76,* 359–380.

Khatskevich, E. (2002). *Soul talk in Russian communication.* Research paper for Communication 794: Cultural discourse analysis. Amherst, MA: University of Massachusetts.

Kidd, K. E. (1986). *Blackfoot ethnography.* Manuscript series No. 8. Edmonton, Alberta: Archaeological Survey of Alberta.

Kipp, D. R. (1993, June). The Blackfeet: A Native American perspective." *Montana Magazine, 119,* 4–11.

Kohlberg, S. (1987). West German and American interactional forms: One level of structured misunderstanding. *Theory, Culture, and Society, 4,* 603–618.

Kotani, M. (2002). Expressing gratitude and indebtedness: Japanese speakers' use of "I'm sorry" in English conversation. *Research on Language and Social Interaction, 35,* 39–72.

Kramer, J. (1990, March 12). Letter from Europe. *The New Yorker, 74,* 76–90.

Krause, A., & Goering, E. (1995). Local talk in the global village: An intercultural comparison of American and German talk shows. *Journal of Popular Culture, 29,* 189–206.

Lange, J. (1993). The logic of competing information campaigns: Conflict over old growth and the spotted owl. *Communication Monographs, 60,* 239–257.

Leeds-Hurwitz, W. (1990). Culture and communication: A review essay. *Quarterly Journal of Speech, 76,* 85–116.

Lehtonen, J.,& Sajavaara, K. (1985). The silent Finn. In D. Tannen & M. Saville-Troike (Eds.), *Perspectives on silence* (pp. 193–201). Norwood, NJ: Ablex.

Lewis, J. (1991). *The ideological octopus: An exploration of television and its audience.* New York: Routledge.

Lewis, O. (1941). Manly-hearted women among the North Peigan. *American Anthropologist, 43.*

Lewis, O. (1942). *The effect of White contact upon Blackfoot culture* (No. 6). Monographs of the American Ethnological Society (A. I. Hallowell, Ed.). New York: J. J. Augustin.

Lewis, R D. (2000). *When cultures collide: Managing successfully across cultures*. London: Nicholas Brealey.

Li, X., & Koole, T. (1998). Cultural keywords in Chinese–Dutch business negotiations. In S. Niemeier, C. Campbell, & R. Dirven (Eds.), *The cultural context in business communication* (pp. 185–213). Amsterdam/Philadelphia: J. J. Benjamin.

Lindlof, T., & Grodin, D. (Eds.). (1996). *Constructing the self in a mediated world*. Thousand Oaks, London, & New Delhi: Sage.

Long Lance. (1928). *Long Lance: The autobiography of a Blackfoot Indian chief by Chicago Buffalo Child Long Lance*. London: Faber.

Long Standing Bear Chief. (1992). *Ni-Kso-Ko-Wa [My Relatives]: Blackfoot spirituality, traditions, values and beliefs*. Browning, MT: Spirit Talk Press.

Lucy, J. (1992). *Language diversity and thought: A reformulation of the linguistic relativity hypothesis*. Cambridge, England: Cambridge University Press.

Manga, J. E. (2003). *Talking trash: The cultural politics of daytime TV talk shows*. New York University Press.

Marsh, D. (1993, December). *The worlds in collision conspiracy. Intercultural situational adaptability as a success factor*. Preston, Lancashire Business, Fifth International Seminar of ENCODE: Languages and Culture: Bridges to International Trade.

Mauranen, A. (1993). *Cultural differences in academic rhetoric*. Frankfurt: Peter Lang Verlag.

McClintock, W. (1992). *The old north trail: Life, legends and religion among the Blackfeet Indians*. Lincoln & London: University of Nebraska Press.

McFee, M. (1968). The 150% man, a product of Blackfeet acculturation. *American Anthropologist, 70,* 1096–1103.

McFee, M. (1977). Modern Blackfeet: Montanans on a reservation. In G. Spindler & L. Spindler (Eds.), *Native North American cultures: Four cases* (pp. 225–360). New York: Holt, Rinehart, & Winston.

Medicine, B. (1994, Winter). North American indigenous women and cultural domination. *Cultural Survival Quarterly, 17,* 66–69.

Milburn, T. (2000). Enacting "Puerto Rican time" in the United States. *International and Intercultural Communication Annual, 23,* 47–76.

Moerman, M. (1988). *Talking culture*. Philadelphia, PA: University of Pennsylvania Press.

Nurmikari-Berry, M., & Berry, M. (1999). Discovering cultural meanings as the first step towards developing intercultural communication competence. In K. Häkkinen (Ed.), *Innovative approaches to intercultural education* (pp. 109–119). University of Jyväskylä, Finland: Publications of Multicultural Programs.

Official publication for the town of Browning and the Blackfeet reservation. (1989, July 6). *Glacier Reporter*, p. 8.

O'Neill, T. D. (1994). Telling about Whites, talking about Indians: Oppression, resistance, and contemporary American Indian identity, *Cultural Anthropology, 9,* 94–126.

Pavlovskaya, A. (1994). *The national image of Russia in intercultural context*. Paper presented at SIETAR Europa Symposium, Jyväskylä, Finland.

Peterson, T. R. (1997). *Sharing the earth: The rhetoric of sustainable development*. Columbia, SC: University of South Carolina Press.

Philips, S. U. (1993). *The invisible culture: Communication in classroom and community on the Warm Springs Indian Reservation*. Prospect Heights, IL: Waveland.

Philipsen, G. (1976). Places for speaking in Teamsterville. *Quarterly Journal of Speech, 62*, 15–25.

Philipsen, G. (1987). The prospect for cultural communication. In L. Kincaid (Ed.), *Communication theory: Eastern and Western perspectives* (pp. 245–254). New York: Academic Press.

Philipsen, G. (1989). Speech and the communal function in four cultures. *International and Intercultural Communication Annual, 13*, 79–92.

Philipsen, G. (1990). An ethnographic approach to communication studies. In B. Dervin, L. Grossberg, B. O'Keefe, & E. Wartella (Eds.), *Rethinking communication: V. 2, paradigm exemplars* (pp. 258–268). Newbury Park, CA: Sage.

Philipsen, G. (1992). *Speaking culturally*. Albany, NY: State University of New York Press.

Philipsen, G. (1997). A theory of speech codes. In G. Philipsen & T. Albrecht (Eds.), *Developing communication theories* (pp. 119–156). Albany, NY: State University of New York Press.

Philipsen, G. (2002). Cultural communication. In W. Gudykunst & B. Mody (Eds.), *Handbook of international and intercultural communication* (pp. 51–67). New York: Sage.

Philipsen, G., & Carbaugh, D. (1986). A bibliography of fieldwork in the ethnography of communication. *Language in Society, 15*, 387–398.

Pomerantz, A. (1978). Compliment responses: Notes on the co-operation of multiple constraints. In J. Shenkein (Ed.), *Studies in the organization of conversational interaction* (pp. 79–112). New York: Academic Press.

Powell, R., & Collier, M. J. (1990). Public speaking instruction and cultural bias. *American Behavioral Scientist, 34*, 240–250.

Priest, P. J. (1995). *Public intimacies: Talk-show participants and tell-all TV*. Cresskill, NJ: Hampton Press.

Rides at the Door, & Davis, D. (1979). *Napi stories*. Browning, MT: Blackfeet Heritage Program.

Rosaldo, M. (1982). The things we do with words: Ilongot speech acts and speech act theory in philosophy. *Language in Society, 11*, 203–237.

Royce, J. (1908). *Race questions, provincialism, and other American problems*. New York: Macmillan.

Sacks, H. (1995). *Lectures on conversation: Volumes I & II* (G. Jefferson, Ed.). Oxford: Blackwell.

Sajavaara, K., & Lehtonen, J. (1997). The silent Finn revisited. In J. Adam (Ed.), *Silence: Interdisciplinary perspectives* (pp. 262–283). New York: Mouton de Gruyter.

Sallinen-Kuparinen, A. (1986). *Finnish communication reticence: Perceptions and self-reported behavior*. Studia Philologica Jyvaskylaensia 19, University of Jyvaskyla, Finland.

Samuels, D. (2001). Indeterminacy and history in Britton Goode's western Apache placenames: Ambiguous identity on the San Carlos Apache reservation. *American Ethnologist, 28*, 277–302.

Schegloff, E. (1995). Introduction. In G. Jefferson (Ed.), *Lectures on conversation: Vols I & II* (p. xxxv). Oxford, England: Blackwell

Schultz, J. W. (1983). *My life as an Indian: The story of a Red woman and a White man in the lodges of the Blackfeet.* Lewis-Clark State College, Lewiston, ID: Confluence Press. (Original work published 1907)

Schultz, J. W. (1962). *Blackfeet and Buffalo: Memories of life among the Indians.* Norman, OK: University of Oklahoma Press.

Schultz, J. W. (1988). *Recently discovered tales of life among the Indians.* Missoula, MT: Mountain Press.

Schultz, J. W., & Donaldson, J. L. (1930). *The sun god's children.* Boston: Houghton Mifflin.

Scollo Sawyer, M. (2004). Nonverbal ways of communicating with nature: A cross-case study. *Environmental Communication Yearbook, 1,* 227–249.

Scollon, R., & Scollon, S. (1981). *Narrative, literacy and face in interethnic communication.* Norwood, NJ: Ablex.

Scollon, R., & Scollon, S. (1995). *Intercultural communication.* Oxford: Blackwell.

Scruton, R. (1979). The significance of common culture. *Philosophy, 54,* 51–70.

Searle, J. (1990). A classification of illocutionary acts. In D. Carbaugh (Ed.), *Cultural communication and intercultural contact* (pp. 349–372). Hillsdale, NJ: Lawrence Erlbaum Associates.

Second Annual Blackfeet Community College traditional encampment. (1989, July 6). *Glacier Reporter,* p. 8.

Sherzer, J. (1987). A discourse-centered approach to language and culture. *American Anthropologist, 89,* 295–309.

Smith, H. (1976). *The Russians.* New York: Ballantine.

Sousa, A. (1994). An "observation" of "participation": Interaction between Cheyenne Americans and Anglo-Americans. Paper prepared for Communication 514: Social Uses of Language, University of Massachusetts, Amherst.

Stokes, R., & Hewitt, J. (1976). Aligning actions. *American Sociological Review, 41,* 838–849.

Tannen, D. (1984). The pragmatics of cross-cultural communication. *Applied Linguistics, 5,* 189–195.

Tannen, D. (1986). Discourse in cross-cultural communication [Special issue]. *Text, 6*(2).

Taylor, T. (1997). *Theorizing language.* New York: Pergamon.

Tolson, A. (Ed.). (2001). *Television talk shows: Discourse, performance, and spectacle.* Mahwah, NJ: Lawrence Erlbaum Associates.

Turner, V. (1980). Social dramas and stories about them. *Critical Inquiry, 7,* 141–168.

Urban, G. (1991). *A discourse-centered approach to culture.* Austin, TX: University of Texas Press.

Walters, A. L. (1992). *Talking Indian: Reflections on survival and writing.* Ithaca, NY: Firebrand Books.

Welch, J. (1974). *Winter in the blood.* New York: Penguin.

Welch, J. (1987a). *Fools crow*. New York: Penguin.

Welch, J. (1987b). *The death of Jim Loney*. New York: Penguin.

Wesaw, M. J. (1994, Winter). Mind over matter: Reflections on the State of the Peoples Tour. *Cultural Survival Quarterly, 17,* 1.

Whorf, B. L. (1956). The relation of habitual thought and behavior to language. In J. Carroll (Ed.), *Language, thought, and reality: selected writings of Benjamin Lee Whorf* (pp. 134–159). Cambridge, MA: The MIT Press.

Wick, N. (1998). Linguistic agons: The self and society opposition and American Quakers. *International and Intercultural Communication Annual, 22,* 100–121.

Wieder, L., & Pratt, S. (1990). On being a recognizable Indian among Indians. In D. Carbaugh (Ed.), *Cultural communication and intercultural contact* (pp. 45–64). Hillsdale, NJ: Lawrence Erlbaum Associates.

Wieder, L., & Pratt, S. (1993). The case of "saying a few words" and "talking for another" among the Osage people: "Public speaking" as an object of ethnography. *Research on Language and Social Interaction, 26,* 353–408.

Wierzbicka, A. (1989). Soul and mind: Linguistic evidence for ethnopsychology and cultural history. *American Anthropologist, 91,* 41–58.

Wilkins, R. (1999). *Asia (matter-of-fact) communication: A Finnish cultural term for talk in educational scenes.* Unpublished doctoral dissertation, University of Massachusetts.

Wissler, C. (1911). *The social life of the Blackfoot Indians.* In *Anthropological papers of the American Museum of Natural History (Vol. 7).* New York: The Trustees.

Wissler, C. (1918). *The sun dance of the Blackfoot Indians.* In *Anthropological papers of the American Museum of Natural History (Vol. 16).* New York: The Trustees.

Wissler, C., & Duvall, D. (1908). *Mythology of the Blackfoot Indians.* In *Anthropological papers of the American Museum of Natural History (Vol. 2).* New York: The Trustees.

Yep, G. (1998). My three cultures: Navigating the multicultural identity landscape. In J. Martin, T. Nakayama, & L. Flores (Eds.), *Readings in cultural contexts* (pp. 79–85). Mountain View, CA: Mayfield.

Source Acknowledgments

Chapter 2 is a revised version of "Cultures in Conversation: Prospects for New World Communities." In D. Marsh and L. Salo-Lee (Eds.), Europe on the Move: Fusion or Fission? (pp. 24–34). Jyvaskyla, Finland: University of Jyvaskyla and SIETAR Europa, 1994.

Chapter 3 (with Saila Poutiainen) is a revised version of "By Way of Introduction: An American and Finnish Dialogue." In M. Lusting and J. Koester (Eds.), *AmongUS: Essays in Identity, Belonging, and Intercultural Competence* (pp. 203–212). New York: Addison and Wesley Longman, 2000.

Chapter 4 is a revised version of "Are Americans really superficial?": Notes of Finnish and American cultures in linguistic action. In L. Salo-Lee (Ed.), *Kieli & Kulttuuri oppimisessa ja opettamisessa* [Language & Culture in Learning and Teaching]. Jyvaskyla: University of Jyvaskyla, Dept. of Communication, 1995; (with Michael Berry). Communicating history, Finnish and American discourses: An ethnographic contribution to intercultural communication inquiry. *Communication Theory, 11*, 352–366, 2001. Used by permission of the International Communication Association and Oxford University Press.

Chapter 5 is a revised version of "Soul" and "self": Soviet and American cultures in conversation. *Quarterly Journal of Speech, 79*, 182–200, 1993. Used by permission of Taylor and Francis (http://www.tandf.co.uk).

Chapter 6 is a revised version of "I can't do that" but I can "actually see around corners": American Indian students and public communication. In J. Lehtonen (ed.), *Critical perspectives on communication research and pedagogy* (pp. 215–234). St. Ingbert, Germany: Rohrig Universitatsverlag, 1995.

144

Chapter 7 is a revised version of "Just listen": Listening and landscape among the Blackfeet. *Western Journal of Communication, 63*(3), 250–270, 1999. Used with permission of the Western Communication Association. Used by permission of the Western States Communication Association.

Index